PENGUIN BOOKS

SOCIOLINGUISTICS: AN INTRODUCTION
TO LANGUAGE AND SOCIETY
Advisory Editor: David Crystal

Peter Trudgill was born in Norwich in 1943, and attended the City of Norwich School. After studying Modern Languages at King's College, Cambridge, he obtained his Ph.D. from the University of Edinburgh in 1971. He taught in the Department of Linguistic Science at the University of Reading from 1970 to 1986, and from 1986 to 1992 at the University of Essex. He is currently Professor of English Linguistics at the University of Lausanne. He has carried out linguistic field-work in Britain, Greece and Norway, and has lectured in most European countries, Canada, the United States, Colombia, Australia, New Zealand, India, Thailand, Hong Kong, Malawi and Japan. Peter Trudgill is the author of: *Accent, Dialect and the School*; *English Accents and Dialects* (with Arthur Hughes); *International English* (with Jean Hannah); *Applied Sociolinguistics*; *Dialects in Contact*; *On Dialect*; *Language in the British Isles*; *Dialectology* (with J.K. Chambers); *The Dialects of England*; *Bad Language* (with Lars Andersson); and other books and articles on sociolinguistics and dialectology.

Sociolinguistics:
An Introduction to Language
and Society

Peter Trudgill

Penguin Books

PENGUIN BOOKS

Published by the Penguin Group
Penguin Books Ltd, 27 Wrights Lane, London W8 5TZ, England
Penguin Books USA Inc., 375 Hudson Street, New York, New York 10014, USA
Penguin Books Australia Ltd, Ringwood, Victoria, Australia
Penguin Books Canada Ltd, 10 Alcorn Avenue, Toronto, Ontario, Canada M4V 3B2
Penguin Books (NZ) Ltd, 182–190 Wairau Road, Auckland 10, New Zealand

Penguin Books Ltd, Registered Offices: Harmondsworth, Middlesex, England

First published in Pelican Books 1974
Revised edition 1983
Reprinted in Penguin Books 1990
Revised edition 1995
10 9 8 7 6 5 4 3

Printed in England by Clays Ltd, St Ives plc
Filmset in 10/12 Monophoto Times by Datix International Ltd, Bungay, Suffolk

Contents

Figures, Maps and Tables

Acknowledgements

A book of this type necessarily draws rather heavily on the work of others. I have made use of the publications of the following scholars without acknowledgement in the text: P. van den Berghe, C. Geertz, J. Gibbons, T. Hill, K. Kazazis, R. Keller, A. Hooper, W. Lockwood, S. Martin, W. McCormack, J. Ornstein, E. Polomé, J. Rubin and W. Stewart. I would like also to acknowledge the help I have had with translations from Ron Brasington, Arne Kjell Foldvik, Viviane Schumacher, and Spanish students at the University of Reading, as well as the invaluable information I have received from Malcolm Petyt, Dubravka Lazić Yarwood, Greek friends, and many other colleagues, students and friends in Reading and elsewhere. I am especially grateful to David Crystal for his help and advice with the book as a whole, and to Jill Tozer for typing it. Thanks are also due to Viv Edwards, Paul Fletcher and Mike Garman for help with the proofs, and to Jean Hannah for her valuable help with the second and third editions. The third edition has also benefited from help and advice from Ian Hancock and David Shaul.

Phonetic Symbols

č	*ch*ew
ç	German i*ch*, Scots ni*ch*t, RP* *hu*ge
ḍ	retroflex† d
ð	*th*is
ɡ	*g*uy
j	*y*ou
ǰ	*j*ust
ḷ	retroflex l
ɽ	retroflex flap, as in some Indian languages and some types of Swedish and Norwegian
ṇ	retroflex n
ṇ	syllabic nasal
ŋ	si*ng*
ɹ	RP *r*ow
R	French *r*ose
š	*sh*e
θ	*th*ing
x	German na*ch*, Scots lo*ch*, Spanish ba*j*o
ž	vi*s*ion
ʔ	a glottal stop, e.g. 'cockney' *better* 'be'er'
ʕ	pharyngeal fricative, as in Arabic
a	French p*a*tte, North of England p*a*t, Australian p*a*rt
ɑ	RP p*a*th, p*a*rt
æ	RP p*a*t

* For the term *RP*, see p. 7.
† For the term *retroflex*, see p. 153.

e	Scots *a*te, French *et*
ɛ	RP b*e*d
ə	*a*bout
ɜ	RP b*i*rd (Note: no [r])
i	RP *ea*t, French *i*l
ɪ	RP *i*t
ɨ	close, central unrounded vowel
o	French *eau*, Scots n*o*
ɔ	RP l*aw*
ɵ	a central vowel between ø and o
ɒ	RP *o*n
ø	French *eux*, German b*ö*se
u	RP f*oo*l, French *ou*
ʊ	RP p*u*ll
ʉ	a central vowel between [y] and [u], cf. Scots 'h*oo*se'
ʌ	RP *u*p
y	French t*u*, German *ü*ber
~	vowel nasalized, e.g. õ
+	vowel fronted, e.g. o̟
.	vowel raised, e.g. o̝
ː	long vowel, e.g. oː

Brackets [ ] indicate phonetic transcription; oblique dashes / /, phonemic transcription.

1. Sociolinguistics – Language and Society

Everyone knows what is supposed to happen when two English people who have never met before come face to face in a train – they start talking about the weather. In some cases this may simply be because they happen to find the subject interesting. Most people, though, are not particularly interested in analyses of climatic conditions, so there must be other reasons for conversations of this kind. One explanation is that it can often be quite embarrassing to be alone in the company of someone you are not acquainted with and *not* speak to them. If no conversation takes place the atmosphere can become rather strained. However, by talking to the other person about some neutral topic like the weather, it is possible to strike up a relationship without actually having to say very much. Train conversations of this kind – and they do happen, although not of course as often as the popular myth supposes – are a good example of the sort of important social function that is often fulfilled by language. Language is not simply a means of communicating information – about the weather or any other subject. It is also a very important means of establishing and maintaining relationships with other people. Probably the most important thing about the conversation between our two English people is not the words they are using, but the fact that they are talking at all.

There is also a second explanation. It is quite possible that the first English person, probably subconsciously, would like to get to know certain things about the second – for instance what sort of job they do and what social status they have. Without this kind of information he or she will not be sure exactly how to behave towards them. The first person can, of course, make intelligent guesses about the second from their clothes, and other visual clues, but can hardly ask direct questions about their social background, at least not at this stage of the relationship. What he or she *can* do – and any reasoning along these lines is again usually subconscious – is to engage them in conversation. The first person is then likely to find out certain things about the other person quite easily. These things will be learnt not so much from what the other person says as from *how it is said*, for whenever we speak we cannot avoid giving our listeners clues about our origins and the sort of person we are. Our accent and our speech generally show where we come from, and what sort of background we have. We may even give some indication of certain of our ideas and attitudes, and all of this information can be used by the people we are speaking with to help them formulate an opinion about us.

These two aspects of language behaviour are very important from a social point of view: first, the function of language in establishing social relationships; and, second, the role played by language in conveying information about the speaker. We shall concentrate for the moment on the second, 'clue-bearing' role, but it is clear that both these aspects of linguistic behaviour are reflections of the fact that there is a close inter-relationship between language and society.

The first English person, in seeking clues about the second, is making use of the way in which people from different social and geographical backgrounds use different kinds of language. If the second English person comes from Norfolk, for example, he or she will probably use the kind of language spoken by people from that part of the country. If the second person is also a middle-class businessman, he will use the kind of language associated with men of this type. 'Kinds of language' of this sort are often referred to as *dialects*, the first type in this case being a regional dialect and the second a social dialect. The term *dialect* is a familiar one and most people will think that they have a good idea of what it means. In fact, though, it is not a particularly easy term to define – and this also goes for the two other commonly used terms which we have already mentioned, *language* and *accent*.

Let us confine our attention for the moment to the terms *dialect* and *language*. Neither represents a particularly clear-cut or watertight concept. As far as *dialect* is concerned, for example, it is possible, in England, to speak of 'the Norfolk dialect' or 'the Suffolk dialect'. On the other hand, one can also talk of more than one 'Norfolk dialect' – 'East Norfolk' or 'South Norfolk', for instance. Nor is the distinction between 'Norfolk dialect' and 'Suffolk dialect' so straightforward as one might think. If you travel from Norfolk into Suffolk, investigating conservative rural dialects as you go, you will find, at least at some points, that the linguistic characteristics of these dialects change *gradually* from place to place. There is no clear *linguistic* break between Norfolk and Suffolk dialects. It is not possible to state in linguistic terms where people stop speaking Norfolk dialect and start speaking Suffolk dialect. There is, that is, a geographical *dialect continuum*. If we choose to place the dividing line between the two at the county boundary, then we are basing our decision on *social* (in this case local-government-political) rather than on linguistic facts.

The same sort of problem arises with the term *language*. For example, Dutch and German are known to be two distinct languages. However, at some places along the Dutch–German frontier the dialects spoken on either side of the border are extremely similar. If we choose to say that people on one side of the border speak German and those on the other Dutch, our choice is again based on social and political rather than linguistic factors. This point is further emphasized by the fact that the ability of speakers from either side of the border to understand each other will often be considerably greater than that of German speakers from this area to understand speakers of other German dialects from distant parts of Austria or Switzerland. Now, in attempting to decide which language someone is speaking, we *could* say that if two speakers cannot understand one another, then they are speaking different languages. Similarly, if they *can* understand each other, we could say that they are speaking dialects of the *same* language. Clearly, however, this would lead to some rather strange results in the case of Dutch and German, and indeed in many other cases.

The criterion of 'mutual intelligibility', and other purely linguistic criteria, are, therefore, of less importance in the use of the terms *language* and *dialect* than are political and cultural factors, of which the two most important are *autonomy* (independence) and *heteronomy* (dependence). We can say that Dutch and German are *autonomous*, since both are independent, standardized varieties of language with, as it were, a life of their own. On the other hand, the nonstandard dialects of Germany, Austria and German-speaking Switzerland are all *heteronomous* with respect to standard German, in spite of the fact that they may be very unlike each other and that some of them may be very like Dutch dialects. This is because speakers of these German dialects look to German as their standard language, read and write in German, and listen to German on radio and television. Speakers of dialects on the Dutch side of the border, in the same way, will read newspapers and write letters in Dutch, and any standardizing changes that occur in their dialects will take place in the direction of Standard Dutch, not Standard German.

A more extreme case which illustrates the sociopolitical nature of these two terms can be taken from Scandinavia. Norwegian, Swedish and Danish are all autonomous, standard languages, corresponding to three distinct nation states. Educated speakers of all three, however, can communicate freely with each other. But in spite of this mutual intelligibility, it would not make sense to say that Norwegian, Swedish and Danish are really the same language. This would constitute a direct contradiction of the political and cultural facts.

This discussion of the difficulty of using purely linguistic criteria to divide up varieties of language into distinct languages or dialects is our first encounter with a problem very common in the study of language and society – the problem of *discreteness* and *continuity*, of whether the division of linguistic and social phenomena into separate entities has any basis in reality, or is merely a convenient fiction. It is as well to point out that this is a problem since terms like 'cockney',

'Brooklynese', 'Yorkshire accent', 'Black dialect' are frequently used as if they were self-evident, self-contained discrete varieties with well-defined, obvious characteristics. It is often convenient to talk as if this were the case, but it should always be borne in mind that the true picture may very well be considerably more complex than this. We can talk, for example, about 'Canadian English' and 'American English' as if they were two clearly distinct entities, but it is in fact very difficult to find any single linguistic feature which is common to all varieties of Canadian English and not present in any variety of American English.

If at this point we return to purely linguistic facts, a further distinction now needs to be made. The term *dialect* refers, strictly speaking, to differences between kinds of language which are differences of vocabulary and grammar as well as pronunciation. The term *accent*, on the other hand, refers solely to differences of pronunciation, and it is often important to distinguish clearly between the two. This is particularly true, in the context of English, in the case of the dialect known as *Standard English*. In many important respects this dialect is different from other English dialects, and some people may find it surprising to see it referred to as a dialect at all. However, in so far as it differs grammatically and lexically from other varieties of English, it is legitimate to consider it a dialect: the term *dialect* can be used to apply to all varieties, not just to nonstandard varieties. (Note that we shall be employing *variety* as a neutral term to apply to any 'kind of language' we wish to talk about without being specific.)

Standard English is that variety of English which is usually used in print, and which is normally taught in schools and to non-native speakers learning the language. It is also the variety which is normally spoken by educated people and used in news broadcasts and other similar situations. The difference between standard and nonstandard, it should be noted, has nothing in principle to do with differences between formal and colloquial language, or with concepts such as 'bad language'. Standard English has colloquial as well as formal variants, and Standard English speakers swear as much as others. (It is worth pointing this out because many people appear to believe that if someone uses slang expressions or informal turns of phrase this means that they are not speaking Standard English.) Historically speaking, the standard language developed out of the English dialects used in and around London as these were modified through the centuries by speakers at the court, by scholars from the universities and other writers, and, later on, by the Public Schools. As time passed, the English used in the upper classes of society in the capital city came to diverge quite markedly from that used by other social groups and came to be regarded as the model for all those who wished to speak and write 'well'. When printing became widespread, it was the form of English most widely used in books, and, although it has undergone many changes, it has always retained its character as the form of the English language with the highest profile.

Within Standard English there are a number of regional differences which tend to attract attention. Standard Scottish English is by no means exactly the same as Standard English English, for example, and Standard American English is somewhat different again. The differences include large numbers of well-known vocabulary items, such as British *lift*, American *elevator*, and some grammatical details:

> British: *I have got.*
> American: *I have gotten.*
> English: *It needs washing.*
> Scottish: *It needs washed.*

There are also a number of other variations associated with smaller regions such as, say, parts of the North and Midlands of England as opposed to the South:

> North: *You need your hair cutting.*
> South: *You need your hair cut.*

Generally speaking, however, Standard English has a widely accepted and codified grammar. There is a general consensus among educated people, and in particular among those who hold powerful and influential positions, as to what is Standard English and what is not – Standard English is, as it were, imposed from above over the range of regional dialects – the dialect continuum – and for this reason can be called a *superposed variety* of language.

This general consensus, however, does not apply to pronunciation. There is no universally acknowledged standard accent for English, and it is, at least in theory, possible to speak Standard English with any regional or social accent. (In practice there are some accents, generally very localized accents associated with groups who have had relatively little education, which do not frequently occur together with Standard English, but there is no necessary connection between Standard English and any particular accent or accents.) There is also one accent which *only* occurs together with Standard English. This is the British English accent, or more properly the English English accent, which is known to linguists as RP ('received pronunciation'). This is the accent which developed largely in the English Public Schools, and which was until recently required of all BBC announcers. It is known colloquially under various names such as 'Oxford English' and 'BBC English', and is still the accent taught to non-native speakers learning British pronunciation.

RP is unusual in that the relatively very small numbers of speakers who use it do not identify themselves as coming from any particular geographical region. RP is largely confined to England, although it also has prestige in the rest of the British Isles (and, to a decreasing extent, in Australia, New Zealand and South Africa). As far as England is concerned, though, RP is a *non-localized* accent. It is, however, not necessary to speak RP to speak Standard English. Standard English can be spoken with any regional accent, and in the vast majority of cases normally is.

Because language as a social phenomenon is closely tied up with the social structure and value systems of society, different dialects and accents are evaluated in different ways. Standard English, for example, has much more status and prestige than any other English dialect. It is a dialect that is highly valued by many people, and certain economic, social and political benefits tend to accrue to those who speak and write it. The RP accent also has very high prestige, as do certain American accents. In fact the 'conventional wisdom' of most English-speaking communities goes further than this. So statusful are Standard English and the prestige accents that they are widely considered to be 'correct', 'beautiful', 'nice', 'pure' and so on. Other nonstandard, non-prestige varieties are often held to be 'wrong', 'ugly', 'corrupt' or 'lazy'. Standard English, moreover, is frequently considered to be *the* English language, which inevitably leads to the view that other varieties of English are some kind of deviation from a norm, the deviation being due to laziness, ignorance or lack of intelligence. In this way millions of people who have English as their mother-tongue are persuaded that they 'can't speak English'.

The fact is, however, that Standard English is only one variety among many, although a peculiarly important one. Linguistically speaking, it cannot even legitimately be considered better than other varieties. The scientific study of language has convinced scholars that *all* languages, and correspondingly *all* dialects, are equally 'good' as linguistic systems. All varieties of a language are structured, complex, rule-governed systems which are wholly adequate for the needs of their speakers. It follows that value judgements concerning the correctness and purity of linguistic varieties are *social* rather than linguistic. There is nothing at all inherent in nonstandard varieties which makes them inferior. Any apparent inferiority is due only to their association with speakers from under-privileged, low-status groups. In other words, attitudes towards non-standard dialects are attitudes which reflect the social structure of society. In the same way, societal *values* may also be reflected in judgements concerning linguistic varieties. For example, it is quite common in heavily urbanized Britain for rural accents, such as those of Devonshire, Northumberland or the Scottish Highlands, to be considered pleasant, charming, quaint or amusing. Urban accents, on the other hand, such as those of Birmingham, Newcastle or London, are often thought to be ugly, careless or unpleasant. This type of attitude towards rural speech is not so widespread in the United States, and this difference may well reflect the different way in which rural life is evaluated in the two countries.

The following example illustrates the extent to which judgements concerning the correctness and purity of linguistic varieties and features are social rather than linguistic. All accents of English have an /r/ sound in words such as *rat* and *rich* and most have an /r/ in *carry, sorry*. On the other hand, there are a number of accents which have no /r/ in words like *cart* and *car*. These words formerly had an /r/ sound, as the spelling shows, but in these accents /r/ has been lost except where it occurs before a vowel. The /r/ in other contexts – at the end of a word (*car*) or before a consonant (*cart*) – can be referred to as 'non-prevocalic /r/'. Accents which lack non-prevocalic /r/ include a number in the United States and West Indies, many in England, Wales and New Zealand, and all in Australia and South Africa. In these accents pairs of words like *ma* and *mar* are pronounced in exactly the same way. Now, if we compare the accents of England and America with respect to this feature, one striking fact emerges. In England, other things being equal, accents *without* non-prevocalic /r/ have more status and are considered more 'correct' than accents *with*. RP, the prestige accent, does not have this /r/, and non-prevocalic /r/ is often used on radio, television and in the theatre to indicate that a character is rural, uneducated or both – one frequently hears it employed for comic effect in radio comedy series. On the other hand, although the situation in the United States is more complex, there are parts of the country where the exact reverse is true. In New York City, other things being equal, accents *with* non-prevocalic /r/ have more prestige and are considered more 'correct' than those without. The pronunciation of words like *car* and *cart* without an /r/ is socially stigmatized, and generally speaking, the higher up the social scale a speaker is, the more non-prevocalic /r/ they are likely to use. In English towns where both types of pronunciation can be heard, such as Bristol and Reading, this pattern is completely reversed. In other words, value judgements about language are, from a linguistic point of view, completely arbitrary. There is nothing inherent in non-prevocalic /r/ that is good or bad, right or wrong, sophisticated or uncultured. Judgements of this kind are social judgements based on the social connotations that a particular feature has in the area in question.

The fact that this is so, however, does not mean that linguists do not acknowledge that society evaluates different linguistic varieties in different ways. Linguistic descriptions note the appropriateness (rather than the 'correctness') of varieties for different contexts, and foreign-language teaching programmes are usually developed to teach the learner the standard variety of a language. At the same time, many linguists believe that the kind of attitude discussed above can in some cases be harmful. For example, it might have undesirable sociopsychological and pedagogical consequences if teachers involved in teaching Standard English to speakers of non-standard varieties appear hostile towards their pupil's speech (see Chapter 9).

Linguists also pay attention to subjective attitudes towards language for other reasons. They are important, for example, in the study of linguistic change, and can often help to explain why a dialect changes when and how it does. An investigation into the speech of New York City has shown that since the Second World War non-prevocalic /r/ has been very much on the increase in the city in the speech of the upper middle class. The impetus for this change may have come from the influx into the city during the war of many speakers from areas where non-prevocalic /r/ was a standard or prestige feature, but the change is more clearly due to a related shift in subjective attitudes towards pronunciations of this type on the part of all New York City speakers. During the course of the investigation tests were carried out on the informants' subjective attitudes in order to see if they reacted to non-prevocalic /r/ as a prestige feature. Those whose response indicated that for them /r/ was a prestige marker were labelled 'r-positive'. Table 1 shows the percentage of upper middle-class speakers in three age-groups who were

Table 1. *Attitudes towards and use of non-prevocalic /r/: upper middle class in New York City*

age	% r-positive informants	% /r/ used
8–19	100	48
20–39	100	34
40 +	62	9

'r-positive' together with the average percentage of non-prevocalic /r/ used in normal speech by the same three groups. It can be seen that for speakers aged under forty there has been a sharp increase in the favourable evaluation of non-prevocalic /r/. There has, correspondingly, been an even sharper increase in the use of this /r/ amongst younger speakers. Other evidence suggests that the change in subjective attitudes has been the cause rather than the effect of the change. The change in subjective attitudes, that is, has led to a change in speech patterns, although it is in fact only the upper middle class which has made a significant change in its speech.

Subjective attitudes towards linguistic forms do not always have this kind of effect. The above example illustrates that if a certain pronunciation comes to be regarded as a prestige feature in a particular community, then it will tend to be exaggerated. This kind of process can also take place in the opposite direction. On Martha's Vineyard, formerly a relatively isolated island off the coast of New England in the United States, fairly dramatic social changes have been taking place as a result of the increasing number of holiday-makers who come to the island in the summer months. These social changes have had linguistic consequences. Investigations have shown that the vowel sound of words such as *house*, *mouth*, *loud* has two different types of pronunciation on the island. (This also applies to the pronunciation of words like *ride* and *right*.) One is a low-prestige, old-fashioned pronunciation typical of the island, approximately [həus], with the first element of the diphthong resembling the vowel in *shirt* or the first vowel in *about*, [əbəut]. The second pronunciation is more recent on the island, and resembles more closely the vowel found in RP and some mainland American prestige accents: [haus], [əbaut]. Strangely enough, work carried out during the 1960s showed that the 'old-fashioned' form appears to be on the increase. The [əu] pronunciation is becoming exaggerated, and is occurring more frequently in the speech of more people. It has emerged that this linguistic change is due to the subjective attitudes speakers on the island have towards this linguistic form. Natives of the island have come to resent the mass invasion of outsiders and the change and economic exploitation that go with it. So those people who most closely identify with the island way of life have begun to exaggerate the typical island pronunciation, in order to signal their separate social and cultural identity, and to underline their belief in the old values. This means that the 'old-fashioned' pronunciation is in fact most prevalent amongst certain sections of the younger community. The tendency is most marked amongst young people who have left to work on the mainland *and have come back* – having rejected the mainland way of life. It is least marked amongst those who have ambitions to settle on the mainland. This process is to a certain extent a conscious one in that speakers are aware of the fact that the island accent is different, but the awareness does not extend to recognition of the significance of the diphthong itself. Unconsciously, however, speakers are aware of the social significance of this pronunciation, and their attitudes towards it are favourable because of their social attitudes. In other words, linguistic change does not always take place in the direction of the prestige norm. On the contrary, all sorts of other attitudes towards language have to be taken into consideration. Language can be a very important factor in group identification, group solidarity and the signalling of difference, and when a group is under attack from outside, signals of difference may become more important and are therefore exaggerated.

In the following chapters we shall examine some of the complex inter-relationships between language and society, of which subjective attitudes are just one facet. These inter-relationships take many forms. In most cases we shall be dealing with the *co-variation* of linguistic and social phenomena. In some cases, however, it makes more sense to consider that the relationship is in one direction only – the influence of society on language, or vice versa. We can begin with an example of this one-way relationship which supposedly involves the effect of language on society. There is a view, developed in various forms by different linguists, which is most frequently referred to as the 'Sapir–Whorf hypothesis', after the two linguists, Edward Sapir and Benjamin Lee Whorf, with whose names it is most often associated. The hypothesis is approximately that speakers' native languages set up series of categories which act as a kind of grid through which they perceive the world, and which constrain the way in which they categorize and conceptualize different phenomena. A language can affect a society by influencing or even controlling the world-view of its speakers. Most languages of European origin are very similar in this respect, presumably because of their common genetic relationship and the long cultural contact between them; the world-views of their speakers and their societies are perhaps for that reason not at all dissimilar. If, therefore, linguistic differences *can* produce cognitive differences, we shall have to demonstrate this by a comparison of sets of very different culturally separated languages.

European languages, for example, make use of tenses. Their usage is by no means identical, but it is usually not too difficult to translate, say, an English form into its equivalent in French or German. Some languages from other parts of the world, on the other hand, do not have tenses, at least not as we know them. They may, however, distinguish in their verb forms between different kinds of activity which European speakers would have to indicate in a much more roundabout way. Verb forms, for instance, may be differentiated according to whether the speaker is reporting a situation or expecting it, and according to an event's duration, intensity, or other characteristics. It would not be too surprising, therefore, if the world-view of a people whose language does not 'have tenses' were rather different from our own: their concept of

time, and perhaps even of cause and effect, might be somewhat different.

A more detailed example will clarify this situation. Consider
the following verb forms from the American Indian language
Hopi:

cami	*camimita*
'it is slashed inwards, from side to side'	'it is fringed'
hari	*haririta*
'it is bent in a rounded angle'	'it lies in a meandering line'
paci	*pacicita*
'it is notched'	'it is serrated'
roya	*royayata*
'it makes a turn'	'it is rotating'

It is interesting, first of all, to speakers of European languages
to see that, for example, 'it is bent' is a verb in Hopi and not
an adjective. The most interesting thing, however, is the way
in which Hopi makes an overt grammatical connection, by
means of a regular linguistic process (repeat the final syllable
and add *ta*), between meanings that we can see are connected,
if we think about it, but which we would not normally see as
being linked. A fringe is indeed a series of slashes; serration
does indeed consist of a number of notches; a meander does
of course consist of a sequence of bends. The thing is that,
because the Hopi language makes available a linguistic way of
making these connections, we can assume that Hopi speakers
will be more aware of these connections than speakers of
languages which do not.

The point of this example is to illustrate that in some cases
differences of language may lead to differences in perception
of the world. It suggests that the Hopi habitually perceive
meaning-relationships of this type in a slightly different way
from English speakers, who have some problems in appreciat-
ing the grammatical connections made in Hopi. However, it is
entirely possible for us to understand the connections. More-

over, translation between Hopi and English is also a perfectly feasible exercise. This indicates that any strong form of the Sapir–Whorf hypothesis – say, that thought is actually constrained by language – cannot be accepted. The example may well be taken to indicate, however, that habitual thought is to a certain extent conditioned by language. English speakers are not normally aware of the semantic connections illustrated above – but constraints of this type can be overcome quite easily if necessary.

The Sapir–Whorf hypothesis is concerned with the possibility that human beings' views of their environment may be conditioned by their language. Less controversial is the one-way relationship that operates in the opposite direction – the effect of society on language, and the way in which environment is reflected in language. First, there are many examples of the *physical* environment in which a society lives being reflected in its language, normally in the structure of its lexicon – the way in which distinctions are made by means of single words. Whereas English, for example, has only one word for *reindeer*, the Sami (Lapp) languages of northern Scandinavia have several. The reasons for this are obvious. It is essential for the Sami to be able to distinguish efficiently between different types of reindeer. English, of course, is quite able to make the same distinctions: *immature reindeer*, *two-year-old reindeer*, and so on, but in the Sami languages this sort of distinction is lexicalized – made by means of individual words.

Secondly, the *social* environment can also be reflected in language, and can often have an effect on the structure of the vocabulary. For example, a society's kinship system is generally reflected in its kinship vocabulary, and this is one reason why anthropologists tend to be interested in this particular aspect of language. We can assume, for example, that the important kin relationships in English-speaking societies are those that are signalled by single vocabulary items: *son, daughter, grandson, granddaughter, brother, sister, father, mother, husband, wife, grandfather, grandmother, uncle, aunt, cousin*. We can, of course, talk of other relationships such as *eldest son, maternal aunt, great uncle*, and *second cousin*, but the distinction between 'maternal' and 'paternal' aunt is not important in our society, and is not reflected in the English lexicon.

This point can be amplified by reference to the kinship vocabularies of other communities. In the Australian aboriginal language Njamal, for example, there are, as in English, fifteen lexicalized kinship distinctions, but the way in which these terms compare with their English equivalents reveals much about the differences between the two societies. The Njamal term *mama* signifies what for the Njamal is a single kinship relationship, but which has to be translated into English in different ways according to context: *father, uncle, male cousin of parent*, and so on. In other words, the term is used for all males of the same generation as the father. For the English speaker, the most striking fact is that the two English words *father* and *uncle* can be translated by one Njamal term. Clearly the distinction between *father* and *father's brother* cannot have the same importance in Njamal society as in our own. On the other hand, whereas English employs the term *uncle* for *father's brother* and *mother's sister's husband*, as well as for *mother's brother* and *father's sister's husband*, Njamal uses *mama* for the first pair and another term, *karna*, for the second. Other Njamal kinship terms distinguish not generation, as in English, but generation distance. For example, a man can use the same term, *maili*, for his *father's father* and his *daughter's son's wife's sister*, the point being that the person in question is two generations removed.

As society is reflected in language in this way, social change can produce a corresponding linguistic change. If, for example, the structure of Njamal society altered radically so that it came to resemble more closely that of English-speaking Australians, we would expect the linguistic system to alter correspondingly. This has happened in the case of Russian. During the period from 1860 to the present day the structure of the Russian kinship system has undergone a very radical change as a result of several important events: the emancipation of serfs in 1861, the First World War, the revolution, the collectivization of agriculture and the Second World War. There has been a marked social as well as political revolution, and this has been accompanied by a corresponding change in the language. For example, in the middle of the last century, *wife's brother* was *shurin*, whereas now it is simply *brat zheny, brother of wife*. Similarly, *brother's wife*, formerly *nevestka*, is now *zhena brata, wife of brother*. In other words, distinctions that were formerly lexicalized, because they were important, are now made by means of phrases. The loss of importance of these particular relationships, and the corresponding linguistic changes, are due to the fact that social changes in Russia have led to the rise of the small, nuclear family. In the last century most Russians lived in large patrilocal extended-family households. Brothers' wives, at that time part of the family, now normally live in different households. Similarly, the term *yatrov*, signifying *husband's brother's wife*, has now disappeared entirely. In earlier days it was a very important reciprocal term, meaning for the woman who used it a person of the same status as herself – a woman from outside married into the father-centred household. As the significance of this status has been lost (not the relationship itself, of course), so has the relevant vocabulary item.

Thirdly, in addition to environment and social structure, the *values* of a society can also have an effect on its language. The most interesting way in which this happens is through the phenomenon known as *taboo*. Taboo can be characterized as being concerned with behaviour which is believed to be supernaturally forbidden, or regarded as immoral or improper; it deals with behaviour which is prohibited or inhibited in an apparently irrational manner. In language, taboo is associated with things which are *not* said, and in particular with words and expressions which are *not* used. In practice, of course, this simply means that there are inhibitions about the normal use of items of this kind – if they were not said at all they could hardly remain in the language.

Taboo words occur in most languages, and failure to adhere to the often strict rules governing their use can lead to punishment or public shame. Many people will never employ words of this type, and most others will only use them in a restricted set of situations. For those who do use taboo words, however, 'breaking the rules' may have connotations of strength or freedom which they find desirable.

Generally, the type of word that is tabooed in a particular language will be a good reflection of at least part of the system of values and beliefs of the society in question. In some communities, word-magic plays an important part in religion, and certain words regarded as powerful will be used in spells and incantations. In different parts of the world taboo words include those for the left hand, for female relations, or for certain game animals. Some words, too, are much more severely tabooed than others. In the English-speaking world, the most severe taboos are now associated with words connected with sex, closely followed by those connected with excretion and the Christian religion. This is a reflection of the great emphasis traditionally placed on sexual morality in our culture. In other, particularly Roman Catholic, cultures the strongest taboos may be associated with religion, and in Norway, for example, some of the most strongly tabooed expressions are concerned with the devil.

Until recently, the strict rules associated with some taboo words in English received legal as well as social reinforcement. Not so long ago, the use in print of words such as *fuck* and *cunt* could lead to prosecution and even imprisonment, and they are still not widely used in newspapers. There is, of course, a certain amount of 'double-think' about words of this type. Although their use was, and may still be, technically illegal in some cases, they occur very frequently in the speech of some sections of the community. This is largely because taboo-words are frequently used as swear-words, which is in turn because they are *powerful*. Most people in modern techno-logically advanced societies would claim not to believe in magic. There is still, however, something that very closely resembles magic surrounding the use of taboo-words in English. The use of taboo-words in non-permitted contexts, such as on television, provokes violent reactions of apparently very real shock and disgust. The reaction, moreover, is an irrational reaction to a particular word, not to a concept. It is perfectly permissible to say 'sexual intercourse' on television. Taboo is therefore clearly a linguistic as well as sociological fact. It is the words themselves which are felt to be wrong and are therefore so powerful.

The strength of this magic is illustrated by the way in which the BBC has on some occasions gone to considerable technical lengths to ensure that telephoned contributions from the public to certain radio programmes broadcast live could be cut off if they contained taboo words. One can infer that they were worried or perhaps even frightened by the prospect of the use of certain words – or the effects of their use. Taboo-words of this type may be in order in certain situations, but they are not yet generally acceptable in the broadcast media.

The phrase 'not yet' indicates the rapidity with which patterns of taboo may change. Legal sanctions against obscene words are disappearing in the English-speaking world and there is a growing tendency for more rational, less magical attitudes to develop towards taboo – 'breaking the rules' is now less dramatic than it used to be, at least in certain situations. A well-known example of this is Shaw's use of *bloody*, now relatively harmless, as a shock-word in *Pygmalion*. Here, too, social change is reflected in a change in linguistic behaviour. On the other hand, as the English-speaking world becomes more sensitive to issues involving inegalitarian discrimination against people on the grounds of their social or physical characteristics, words such as *nigger, cripple, poof* are acquiring increased taboo-loading, and their use is becoming increasingly shocking.

A further interesting point is the secondary effect that taboo can have on language itself. Because of the strong reluctance of speakers to utter taboo words, or words like them, in certain circumstances, words which are phonetically similar to taboo words can be lost from a language. It is often said, for example, that *rabbit* replaced the older word *coney* (pronounced [kʌni]) in English for this reason. A similar explanation is advanced for the widespread American use of *rooster* rather than *cock*. In the case of bilingual individuals, this can even take place across languages, apparently. American Indian girl speakers of Nootka have been reported by teachers to be entirely unwilling to use the English word *such* because of the close phonetic resemblance it bears to the Nootka word for *vagina*. Similarly, Thai students in England are said to avoid the use of Thai words such as [kha:n] 'to crush' when speaking Thai in the presence of English speakers, in the belief that this could cause offence.

These, then, are some of the ways in which society acts upon language and, possibly, in which language acts upon society. We have seen that there are a number of ways in which language and society are inter-related, and in the following chapters we shall investigate some further aspects of this kind of inter-relationship. In the past thirty years or so, increasing recognition of the importance of this relationship has led to the growth of a relatively new sub-discipline within linguistics: *sociolinguistics*. It is a broad but fair generalization to say that much of linguistics in the past completely ignored the relationship between language and society. In most cases this was for good reasons. Concentration on the 'idiolect' – the speech of one person at one time in one style – was a necessary simplification that led to several theoretical advances. However, as we have already indicated, language is very much a social phenomenon. A study of language totally without reference to its social context inevitably leads to the omission of some of the more complex and interesting aspects of language and to the loss of opportunities for further theoretical progress. One of the main factors that has led to the growth of sociolinguistic research has been the recognition of the importance of the fact that language is a very variable phenomenon, and that this variability may have as much to do with society as with language. A language is not a simple, single code used in the same manner by all people in all situations, and linguists now understand that it is both possible and beneficial to try to tackle this complexity.

Sociolinguistics, then, is that part of linguistics which is concerned with language as a social and cultural phenomenon. It investigates the field of language and society and has close connections with the social sciences, especially social psychology, anthropology, human geography, and sociology. The study of attitudes to forms of language, such as the use of non-prevocalic /r/, is an example of the sort of work carried out under the heading of the *social psychology of language*. The study of Njamal kinship terms, on the other hand, is a good example of *anthropological linguistics*, while the study of the way in which dialects vary gradually from one region to another, as from Norfolk to Suffolk, or from the Netherlands to Germany, comes under *geolinguistics*, as do a number of topics we shall be discussing in Chapter 8. Chapter 6 deals with aspects of *discourse analysis* and the *ethnography of speaking*. In Chapter 7 'Language and Nation', Chapter 9 'Language and Humanity', and elsewhere, we shall be dealing with topics under the heading of the *sociology of language*, which deals with the study of who speaks which language (or variety) to whom, and with the application of these findings to social, political and educational problems. And throughout the book we shall be concerned with what some writers have referred to as 'secular linguistics' and others as 'sociolinguistics proper'. This covers studies of language in its social context – language as spoken by ordinary people in their everyday lives – which are mainly concerned with answering questions of interest to linguists, such as how and why language changes (we have already noted insights into linguistic change obtained from the New England and New York studies) and how we can improve our theories about the nature of language.

2. Language and Social Class

If you are an English-speaker you will be able to estimate the relative social status of the following speakers solely on the basis of the linguistic evidence given here:

Speaker A	Speaker B
I done it yesterday.	*I did it yesterday.*
He ain't got it.	*He hasn't got it.*
It was her what said it.	*It was her that said it.*

If you heard these speakers say these things you would guess that B was of higher social status than A, and you would almost certainly be right. How is it that we are able to do this sort of thing?

The answer lies in the existence of varieties of language which have come to be called *social-class dialects*. There are grammatical differences between the speech of these two speakers which give us clues about their social backgrounds. It is also probable, although this is not indicated on the printed page, that these differences will be accompanied by phonetic and phonological differences – that is to say, there are also different *social-class accents*. The internal differentiation of human societies is reflected in their languages. Different social groups use different linguistic varieties, and as experienced members of a speech community we (and our English person on the train) have learnt to classify speakers accordingly.

Why does social differentiation have this effect on language? We may note parallels between the development of these social varieties and the development of regional varieties: in both cases *barriers* and *distance* appear to be relevant. Dialectologists have found that regional-dialect boundaries often coincide with *geographical* barriers, such as mountains, swamps or rivers: for example, all local-dialect speakers in the areas of Britain north of the river Humber (between Lincolnshire and Yorkshire) still have a monophthong in words like *house* ('*hoose*' [huːs]), whereas speakers south of the river have had some kind of [haus]-type diphthong for several hundred years. It also seems to be the case that the greater the geographical distance between two dialects the more dissimilar they are linguistically: for instance, those regional varieties of British English which are most unlike the speech of London are undoubtedly those of the north-east of Scotland – Buchan, for example. The development of social varieties can perhaps be explained in the same sort of way – in terms of *social* barriers and *social* distance. The diffusion of a linguistic feature through a society may be halted by barriers of social class, age, race, religion or other factors. And social distance may have the same sort of effect as geographical distance: a linguistic innovation that begins amongst, say, the highest social group will affect the lowest social group last, if at all. (We must be careful, however, not to explain all social differences of language in these entirely mechanical terms since, as we saw in Chapter 1, *attitudes* to language clearly play an important role in preserving or removing dialect differences.)

Of the many forms of social differentiation, for example by class, age, sex, race or religion, we shall concentrate in this chapter on the particular type of social differentiation illustrated in the example of speakers A and B – *social stratification*. Social stratification is a term used to refer to any hierarchical ordering of groups within a society. In the industrialized societies of the West this takes the form of stratification into social classes, and gives rise linguistically to social-class dialects. (The whole question of social class is in fact somewhat controversial, especially since sociologists are not agreed as to the exact nature, definition or existence of social classes. There is little point, however, in attempting to list or evaluate here the different approaches adopted by sociological theorists to this topic. Suffice it to say that social classes are

Table 2. Regional and caste differences in Kanarese

| | Brahmin | | non-Brahmin | |
	Dharwar	Bangalore	Dharwar	Bangalore
'it is'	ədə	ide	ayti	ayti
'inside'	-olage	-alli	-āga	-āga
infinitive affix	-likke	-ōk	-āk	-āk
participle affix	-ō	-ō	-ā	-ā
'sit'	kūt-	kūt-	kunt-	kunt-
reflexive	kō	kō	kont-	kont-

generally taken to be aggregates of individuals with similar social and/or economic characteristics. The general attitude adopted towards social class in most linguistic studies will emerge from the following paragraphs.)

Social-class stratification is not universal, however. In India, for example, traditional society is stratified into different *castes*. As far as the linguist is concerned, *caste dialects* are in some ways easier to study and describe than social-class dialects. This is because castes are relatively stable, clearly named groups, rigidly separated from each other, with hereditary membership and with little possibility of movement from one caste to another. (This is a considerable simplification of the actual situation, but my main point is to emphasize the difference between caste and class societies.) Because of this rigid separation into distinct groups, caste-dialect differences tend to be relatively clear-cut, and social differences in language are sometimes greater than regional differences. Table 2 illustrates these points with data from Kanarese, a Dravidian language of south India. It shows a number of forms used by Brahmins, the highest caste, and their equivalents in the speech of the lower castes, in two towns, Bangalore and Dharwar, which are about 250 miles apart.

The first three examples show that, although the Bangalore and Dharwar forms are the same for the lower castes, the Brahmin caste has forms which are not only different from the other castes but also *different from each other* in the two towns. The higher-caste forms are more localized than the lower-caste forms. (We shall see that the reverse is true of class varieties of English.) The second three examples show that there is more similarity within social than geographical groups – social distance is more differentiating than geographical distance.

In the class societies of the English-speaking world the social situation is much more fluid, and the linguistic situation is therefore rather more complex, at least in certain respects. Social classes are not clearly defined or labelled entities but simply aggregates of people with similar social and economic characteristics; and social mobility – movement up or down the social hierarchy – is perfectly possible. This makes things much more difficult for any linguist who wishes to describe a particular variety – the more heterogeneous a society is, the more heterogeneous is its language. For many years the linguist's reaction to this complexity was generally to ignore it – in two rather different ways. Many linguists concentrated their studies on the *idiolect* – the speech of one person at one time in one style – which was thought (largely erroneously, as it happens – see p. 28) to be more regular than the speech of the community as a whole. Dialectologists, on the other hand, concentrated on the speech of rural informants, and in particular on that of elderly people of little education or travel experience, in small isolated villages. Even small villages are socially heterogeneous, of course, but it is easier to ignore this fact in villages than in large towns.

It is only fair to say, however, that there are two additional explanations for why dialectologists concentrated on rural areas in this way. First, they were concerned to record many dialect features which were dying out before they were lost for ever. Secondly, there was a feeling that hidden somewhere in the speech of older, uneducated people were the 'real' or 'pure' dialects which were steadily being corrupted by the standard variety, but which the dialectologists could discover and describe if they were clever enough. (It turns out that the 'pure' homogeneous dialect is also largely a mythical concept:

all language is subject to stylistic and social differentiation, because all human communities are functionally differentiated and heterogeneous to varying degrees. All language varieties are also subject to change. There is, therefore, an element of differentiation even in the most isolated conservative rural dialect.) Gradually, however, dialectologists realized that by investigating only the speech of older, uneducated speakers they were obtaining an imperfect and inaccurate picture of the speech of different areas. (For example, the records of the Survey of English Dialects show that the county of Surrey, immediately to the south of London, is an area where non-prevocalic /r/ is pronounced in words like *yard* and *farm* (see p. 147) whereas anybody who has been to Surrey will know that this is simply not the case for a large proportion of the population.)

Dialectologists then began to incorporate social as well as geographical information into their dialect surveys. For example, workers on the Linguistic Atlas of the United States and Canada, which was begun in the 1930s, divided their informants into three categories largely according to the education they had received, and thereby added a social dimension to their linguistic information. They also began, in a rather tentative kind of way, to investigate the speech of urban areas. It was not really until after the Second World War, however, that linguists also began to realize that in confining dialect studies to mainly rural areas they were remaining singularly ignorant about the speech of the vast majority of the population – those who lived in towns. A large amount of linguistic data that was both interesting in itself and potentially valuable to linguistic theory was being ignored or lost. For this reason, works with titles like *The Speech of New York City* and *The Pronunciation of English in San Francisco* began to appear. Urban studies presented a further problem, however – how on earth could a linguist describe 'the speech of New York City' – a city of eight million or more inhabitants? How accurate was it to refer to the 'English in San Francisco' when your work was based on the analysis of the speech of only a small number of the tens of thousands of speakers you could have investigated? Was it, in other words, legitimate or worthwhile to apply the methods of traditional rural dialectology to large urban areas? The answer was eventually seen to be 'No'.

Those urban dialectologists who recognized that this was the case were therefore forced to work out how they were to describe, *fully* and *accurately*, the speech of large towns and cities, and it was in response to this problem that urban dialectology eventually became sociolinguistic. In 1966, the American linguist, William Labov, published in *The Social Stratification of English in New York City* the results of a large-scale survey of the speech of New York. He had carried out tape-recorded interviews, not with a handful of informants, but with 340. Even more important, his informants were selected, not through friends or personal contacts (as had often been the case earlier), but by means of a scientifically designed random sample, which meant that though not everybody could be interviewed, everybody had an equal *chance* of selection for interview. By bringing sociological methods such as random sampling to linguistics, Labov was able to claim that the speech of his informants was truly representative of that of New York (or at least of the particular area he investigated, the Lower East Side). Since the informants were a representative sample, the linguistic description could therefore be an *accurate* description of *all* the varieties of English spoken in this area. Labov also developed techniques, later refined, for eliciting normal speech from people in spite of the presence of the tape-recorder. (This was an important development which we shall discuss further in Chapter 5.) He also developed methods for the quantitative measurements of linguistic data, which will be described in part below. Since this breakthrough many other studies of urban dialects have been made, in many parts of the world, on the same sort of pattern.

The methods developed by Labov have proved to be very significant for the study of social-class dialects and accents. The methods of traditional dialectology may be adequate for the description of caste dialects (though even this is doubtful) since any individual, however selected, stands a fair chance of being not too different from the caste group as a whole. But it is not possible to select individual speakers and to generalize from them to the rest of the speakers in their social-class group. This was an important point that was demonstrated by Labov. The speech of single speakers (their idiolects) may differ considerably from those of others like them. Moreover, it may also be internally very inconsistent. The speech of most New Yorkers appeared to vary in a completely random and unpredictable manner. Sometimes they would say *guard* with an /r/, sometimes without. Sometimes they would say *beard* and *bad* in the same way, sometimes they would make a difference. Linguists have traditionally called this 'free variation'. Labov showed, however, that the variation is not free. Viewed against the background of the speech community as a whole, the variation was not random but determined by extra-linguistic factors in a quite predictable way. That is, the researcher could not predict on any one occasion whether individuals would say *cah* or *car*, but he could show that, if they were of a certain social class, age and sex, they would use one or other variant approximately x per cent of the time, on average, in a given situation. The idiolect might appear random, but the speech community was quite predictable. In any case, by means of methods of the type employed by Labov the problem of the heterogeneity of speech communities has been, at least partly, overcome. We are now able to correlate linguistic features with social class accurately, and obtain thereby a clearer picture of social dialect differentiation.

As far as English is concerned, linguists have known for a long time that different dialects and accents are related to differences of social-class background. In Britain, we can describe the situation today in the following, somewhat simplified way. Conservative, and, in particular, rural dialects – old-fashioned varieties associated with groups lowest in the social hierarchy – change gradually as one moves across the countryside. The point made in Chapter 1 about travelling from Norfolk into Suffolk is equally valid for a journey from Cornwall to Aberdeen: there exists a whole series of differ-

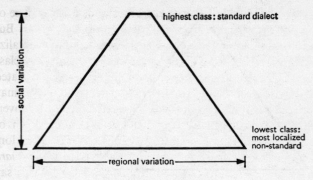

Figure 1. Social and regional dialect variation

ent dialects which gradually merge into one another. This series is referred to as a *dialect continuum* – a large number of different but not usually distinct nonstandard dialects connected by a chain of similarity, but with the dialects at either end of the chain being very dissimilar. At the other end of the social scale, however, the situation is very different. Speakers of the highest social class employ the dialect we have called Standard English, which, as we saw in Chapter 1, is only very slightly different in different parts of the country. The situation can therefore be portrayed as in Figure 1. To take a lexical example, there is in the Standard English dialect a single word *scarecrow* signifying the humanoid object farmers place in fields to scare off birds. At the other end of the pyramid, on the other hand, we find a far greater degree of regional variation in the most localized regional English dialects. Corresponding to *scarecrow* we have *bogle, flay-crow, mawpin, mawkin, bird-scarer, moggy, shay, guy, bogeyman, shuft, rook-scarer,* and several others. The same sort of pattern is also found with grammatical differences. In Standard English, for example, we find both:

> *He's a man who likes his beer.* and
> *He's a man that likes his beer.*

But regional variation in nonstandard varieties is much greater. All the following are possible:

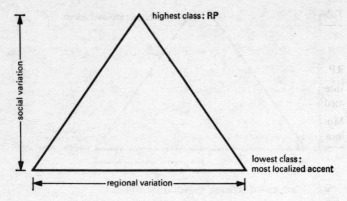

Figure 2. Social and regional accent variation

> *He's a man who likes his beer.*
> *He's a man that likes his beer.*
> *He's a man at likes his beer.*
> *He's a man as likes his beer.*
> *He's a man what likes his beer.*
> *He's a man he likes his beer.*
> *He's a man likes his beer.*

As far as accent is concerned, the situation is slightly different, as portrayed in Figure 2, because of the unique position of RP. (This is not to say that there is no variation within RP, but what there is is generally not regionally determined.) This means that at any given point in England, and at least in parts of the rest of the United Kingdom, there is a continuum of accents ranging from RP, through various local accents, to the most localized accent associated with the lowest social class. Table 3 illustrates this situation as it affects the pronunciation of one word, *home*. In the top line of this table there is only one variant, while there are eight on the bottom line. In the second line, moreover, the presence of [hoːm] in both Edinburgh and Newcastle, and, particularly, of [hoʊm] in both Liverpool and Bradford, indicates the way in which certain non-RP pronunciations acquire the status of less locally restricted, regional standard pronunciations in various parts of the country.

Table 3. RP and local-accent pronunciation of home

	Edinburgh	Newcastle	Liverpool	Bradford	Dudley	Norwich	London
RP	həʊm	həʊm	həʊm	həʊm	həʊm	həʊm	həʊm
Intermediate	hoːm	hoːm huom	houm	hoʊm hɔːm	hɔʊm ɔʊm	huːm hʊm	hʌʊm ʌʊm
Most localized	heːm	hiem jem	oʊm	ɔːm	wʊm	ʊm	æʊm

We have known for a long time about this kind of social and regional dialect and accent variation, and we have also been fairly well provided with descriptions of RP. We have not known, however, exactly how RP and the intermediate and most localized accents are related to social class; how far RP extends down the social scale in different places; what kind of speaker uses the regional standard pronunciation; and exactly what the intermediate and localized accents are like. Linguists are now in a position to begin to answer these questions.

If we are to obtain a correct picture of the relationship between language and social stratification we must be able to *measure* both linguistic and social phenomena so that we can correlate the two accurately. As far as social class is concerned this can be done relatively easily (it is still far from simple) by the sociological method of assigning individuals a numerical index score on the basis of their occupational, income, educational and/or other characteristics, and then grouping them together with others with similar indexes (although the justification for different groupings may be controversial). Measuring language is more difficult. The solution developed by Labov and since used by others is to take linguistic features which are known, either from previous study or intuitively by the linguist as a native speaker, to vary within the community being studied, and which are also easily countable in some way. For instance, in two separate surveys, one in Detroit, USA, and one in Norwich, England, the same grammatical

Table 4. Verbs without -s in Norwich and Detroit

Norwich		Detroit	
MMC	0%	UMC	1%
LMC	2	LMC	10
UWC	70	UWC	57
MWC	87	LWC	71
LWC	97		

feature appeared to be suitable in this way. In Standard English the third-person present-tense singular form of verbs has an affix, orthographic -*s*, which distinguishes it from other persons: *I know, we know, they know*, but *she knows*. In East Anglia, the area of England in which Norwich is situated, and in Detroit this -*s* is often not present, at least in the speech of some people. This means that the following sorts of forms occur:

> *She like him very much.*
> *He don't know a lot, do he?*
> *It go ever so fast.*

Since Standard English has the -*s*, and since the standard variety is generally most closely associated with higher social groups, it was suspected that there might be a direct correlation between social-class position and usage of -*s*. To investigate this possibility was relatively easy, since there was no difficulty in measuring this linguistic feature: it was simply a matter of listening to tape-recordings made during the surveys and counting the number of times a speaker did or did not use -*s*. Table 4 shows the results of these investigations for Norwich speakers and for Black speakers in Detroit. The table shows that the suspicion is quite justified – there is a clear correlation between social class and usage of -*s*. (Norwich informants have been divided into five social-class groups – middle middle class; lower middle class; upper working class; middle working class; and lower working class – on the basis of their social-class index scores. The linguists working with the Detroit informants divided them into four social-class groups.)

The relationship is obvious – but what exactly is the value of this kind of information? First, it shows precisely what sort of information we are working with when we assign a social status to a speaker on the basis of linguistic evidence. Through our linguistic experiences we have become sensitive, normally subconsciously, to correlations of this type between social class and standard or local linguistic forms. Secondly, it tells us a little about the social structure of the two communities. In both cases, by far the biggest gap between any two scores is that between the LMC and the UWC. This suggests that the division of society into two main class groups, 'middle class' and 'working class', a division made largely but not entirely on the basis of the difference between manual and non-manual occupations, is of some validity and importance, since the social barrier is clearly reflected in language. Thirdly, it illustrates the point made above about the idiolect. Although individuals will sometimes use one verb form, and sometimes another, the average percentage for each group falls into a quite predictable pattern.

Finally, it tells us a lot about social-class dialects. Even though we are concentrating on only one feature rather than on a variety as a whole, it is still apparent that, like regional dialects, social-class dialects are not distinct entities. They merge into each other to form a continuum. We can if we like talk of 'the middle-working-class Norwich dialect', but if we do we must be very clear (a) that our division into five social classes may be arbitrary; (b) that the linguistic differences involved are simply relative and involve the frequency of occurrence of particular features; and (c) there may be differing results if other linguistic variables are taken. Popular stereotypes of social-class dialects are therefore almost always misleading: it is not accurate, for example, to make statements like, 'The Detroit Black dialect has no third-person marker on present-tense verbs.' Detroit Blacks of all social classes use forms both of the *it go* and of the *it goes* type – it is only the proportions which are different.

Now, the situation portrayed in both the above cases could be regarded as being a case of *dialect mixture*. We could say, that is, that in the first case what we are *really* faced with is two different dialects, one with and one without the *-s*. (The Norwich MMC score gives some support to this view.) We could then state that these two separate dialects are mixed in different proportions by speakers from different classes. This may in fact be a valid historical explanation of how this situation arose in the first place. In my view, however (and not all linguists would agree with me), it is better to describe the present-day situation as a case of *inherent variability* (at least in Norwich – the position in Detroit is less clear). *Inherent variability* means that the variation is not due to the mixture of two or more varieties but is an integral part of the variety itself. Thus according to the 'dialect-mixture view' Detroit Black speakers vary their verb forms because they mix Detroit Black English (which in its 'pure' form does not have *-s*) with Standard English (which does). According to the 'inherent-variability view', on the other hand, this variation is simply one characteristic of Detroit Black English. The evidence for this second view is that this kind of variation takes place on a very wide scale, involving all speakers and a very large number of other linguistic features. More tellingly, this kind of variability is found even in the speech of very young children who have not been exposed to other dialects. Linguistic varieties appear to be inherently variable as a rule rather than as an exception, and inherent variability is probably the linguistic counterpart of social heterogeneity.

A number of other, rather more complex grammatical features have also been shown to correlate with social class in the same kind of patterned manner – to characterize, by their frequency of occurrence, different (but non-discrete) class dialects. Consider, for example, what happens if we wish to negate the following sentence:

I can eat anything.

There are two possibilities in the standard variety of English. We can either negate the verb, to produce:

I can't eat anything.

or we can negate the pronoun:

I can't eat nothing.

(The same is true of other similar sentences containing an indefinite article or indefinite pronoun.) There are other varieties of English, however, where there is a third possibility – where we can negate both elements:

I can't eat nothing.

It was found in the Detroit survey that there was a clear relationship, again of the relative-frequency type, between employment of the third possibility – *double* or, better, *multiple negation* – and social class. The percentages of non-standard forms used were:

UMC	2
LMC	11
UWC	38
LWC	70

– again we have the same sort of class pattern, and again no single class consistently uses only one form or the other.

Social-class *accents*, in contrast to grammatical features, appear rather more difficult to handle. We know, from our experience as native speakers, that there are a whole range of socially determined accents, but how exactly are we to correlate these phonetic and phonological features with sociological parameters? The usual method is to investigate, singly, the pronunciation of individual vowels and consonants. It is, for example, relatively simple to count the presence or absence of particular consonants in any stretch of speech. In Norwich the following three features were studied:

1. the percentage of *n'* as opposed to *ng* in *walking, running*, etc. – [wɔːkn̩] versus [wɔːkɪŋ].

2. the percentage of glottal stops as opposed to *t* in *butter, bet*, etc. – [bʌʔə] versus [bʌtə].

3. the percentage of 'dropped *h*s' as opposed to *h* in *hammer, hat*, etc. – [æmə] versus [hæmə].

Table 5. Non-RP forms for three consonants in Norwich

	1. *ng*	2. *t*	3. *h*
MMC	31%	41%	6%
LMC	42	62	14
UWC	87	89	40
MWC	95	92	59
LWC	100	94	61

The results are shown in Table 5. The three consonants are clearly good indicators of social-class position in Norwich, and are particularly significant as indicators of membership of the middle-class or working-class as a whole. Once again, moreover, it seems that it is not possible to talk legitimately of discrete social-class accents – again there is a continuum, with most speakers using sometimes one pronunciation, sometimes another. (This means, of course, that Table 3 on p. 31 is a rather crude representation of the facts.) The vast majority of Norwich speakers use both pronunciations of all three consonants. It is also particularly interesting to note that even the highest class uses *walkin'*-type pronunciations 31 per cent of the time, on average.

Probably the first study of consonantal variation of this kind was made by Labov in New York City, prior to his main survey. The hypothesis that non-prevocalic /r/ usage would be correlated with social class was tested in an experiment rather more amusing than many linguistic investigations – by examining the speech of shop assistants in three different department stores, of high, medium and low status respectively. The procedure was to find out which departments were on the fourth floor and then to ask as many assistants as possible in the rest of the shop a question like, 'Excuse me, where are the women's shoes?' The answer to this would be *fourth floor* – with two possible occurrences of non-prevocalic /r/. In this way information on /r/-usage was obtained from 264 informants (who did not know, of course, that they were being interviewed by a linguist). The results were: 38 per cent of the high-ranking store assistants used no /r/, 49 per cent in

Table 6. New York vowels in bad

1.	[brᵊd]	cf. RP, NYC *beard*
2.	[bɛᵊd]	cf. RP, NYC *bared*
3.	[bæːd]	cf. North of England *bed*
4.	[bæːd]	cf. RP *bad*

the middle store and 83 per cent in the low-ranking store. Thus, as well as acquiring a vast amount of rather restricted knowledge about the topography of New York department stores, the investigator obtained an important indication of how socially significant a relatively trivial feature of accent can be.

With vowels, which are often socially more significant than consonants, the problem of measurement is greater, since it is not the presence or absence of a particular sound which is involved, but small (often very small) differences of vowel quality. The linguist gets round this problem by distinguishing accurately (although often arbitrarily) between different vowel qualities and treating them as though they were discrete sounds. For example, there is a wide range of socially significant variation in New York English in the pronunciation of the vowel in *cab, bag, bad, half, path, dance*. The different variants form a continuum, but it is possible to split this up artificially, as in Table 6, into four distinct types. An index score can then be calculated for each individual (and then for each class group) by calculating the average of the values assigned to each occurrence of this vowel in their speech. This will indicate the *average* pronunciation an individual or group uses – if individuals consistently say *bad, bag, half* as [brᵊd] etc. they will score 1.0, whereas if they consistently say [bæːd] they will score 4.0. Results for three social-class groups were as follows:

UC	2.7
MC	2.5
LC	2.3

Thus, in casual conversation, all New Yorkers use on average a pronunciation between [bɛᵊd] and [bæːd], but there is a small but consistent difference between the social classes: lower-class speakers tend to use a closer vowel more frequently than higher-class speakers. A very small vowel-quality difference therefore turns out to be socially rather significant.

The same sort of technique has been used in the analysis of British accents. In Norwich English it is possible to distinguish three different vowel qualities in words such as *pass, part, shaft, bath, card*: 1 is the long back vowel [aː] of RP *pass* or American *pot*, 2 is an intermediate vowel, and 3 is a front vowel [aː] similar to the vowel in Australian or eastern New England *part*. This means that scores can range from 1.0 for a consistent RP pronunciation to 3.0 for consistent use of the frontal vowel. The correlation of vowel quality with social class works out as follows:

MMC	1.9
LMC	2.1
UWC	2.8
MWC	2.9
LWC	3.0

Generally, WC speakers have a front vowel in Norwich English, while MC speakers have a central vowel, but there are still, on average, fine differences of vowel quality which distinguish one class from another. Many other class differences of the same kind could be cited from almost any area you care to name. In Leeds, England, for example, middle-class speakers tend to have a vowel of the [ʌ] type in words such as *but, up, fun*, while working-class speakers have a higher, rounder vowel, [ʊ]; in London, *name, gate, face*, etc. are pronounced [neɪm], [nɛɪm], or [næɪm] depending on social class (highest-class form first); in Chicago the vowel of *roof, tooth, root* is most often [u] but is frequently more centralized [ʉ] in the speech of members of higher social-class groups; and in Boston, Massachusetts, upper-class speakers have [ɵʊ] in *ago, know*, while other speakers have [oʊ].

3. Language and Ethnic Group

An experiment was carried out in the USA in which a number of people acting as judges were asked to listen to tape-recordings of two different sets of speakers. Many of the judges decided that speakers in the first set were black, and speakers in the second set white – and they were completely wrong, since it was the first set which consisted of white people, and the second of Blacks. But they were wrong in a very interesting way. The speakers they had been asked to listen to were exceptional people: the white speakers were people who had lived all their lives amongst Blacks, or had been raised in areas where black cultural values were dominant; the black speakers were people who had been brought up, with little contact with other Blacks, in predominantly white areas. The fact was that the white speakers *sounded* like Blacks, and the black speakers *sounded* like Whites – and the judges listening to the tape-recordings reacted accordingly. This experiment demonstrates two rather important points. First, there are differences between the English spoken by many Whites and many Blacks in America such that Americans can, and do, assign people with some confidence to one of the two ethnic groups solely on the basis of their language – this might happen in a telephone conversation, for instance – which suggests that 'black speech' and 'white speech' have some kind of social reality for many Americans. This has been confirmed by other experiments, carried out in Detroit, which have shown that Detroiters of all ages and social classes have an approximately eighty per cent success rate in recognizing black or white speakers (from unexceptional backgrounds in this test) on the basis of only a few seconds of tape-recorded material. Secondly, the experiment demonstrates rather convincingly that, although the stereotypes of black or white speech which listeners work with provide them with a correct identification most of the time, the diagnostic differences are entirely the result of *learned* behaviour. People do not speak as they do *because* they are white or black. What does happen is that speakers acquire the linguistic characteristics of those they live in close contact with. Members of the two American ethnic groups we have been discussing learn the linguistic varieties associated with them in exactly the same way that social-class dialects are acquired, and in those unusual cases where Whites live amongst Blacks, or vice versa, the pattern acquired is that of the locally predominant group.

This means – and it may perhaps *still* be necessary to emphasize this – that there is no racial or physiological basis of any kind for linguistic differences of this type. In the past, of course, it was quite widely believed that there was or might be some connection between language and race. For example, during the nineteenth century, the originally linguistic term *Indo-European* came also to have racial connotations. The term *Indo-European* was coined to cover those languages of Europe, the Middle East and India which, linguists had discovered, were historically related to each other. Subsequently, however, a myth grew up of an imaginary Indo-European or Aryan race who had not only spoken the parent Indo-European language but who were also the ancestors of the Germans, Romans, Slavs and of others who now speak Indo-European languages. Unfortunately for adherents of this view, any human being can learn any human language, and we know of many well-attested cases of whole ethnic groups switching language through time – one has only to think, for example, of the large numbers of people of African origin who now speak originally European languages. There can, therefore, be no guarantee whatsoever – indeed, it is exceptionally unlikely – that groups of people are 'racially related' because they speak related languages. We cannot say that Slavs and Germans are physically, genetically related simply because they speak related Indo-European languages.

Ideas about languages and race die hard, however. The German language, for instance, was an important component of the Nazis' theories about the Germanic 'master race'; and false ideas about the possibility and desirability of preserving 'linguistic purity' (i.e. defending a language against 'contamination' by loan words from other languages) may go hand in hand with equally false ideas about racial purity. Perhaps less harmful, but probably much more persistent, are references to, for example, the Romanians as a 'Latin' people (with all kinds of implications about 'national character') for no other reason than that they speak a Romance language. It is true, of course, that Rumanian represents a historical development of Latin (with a considerable admixture from Slavic and other languages), but it simply does not follow that Romanians are 100 per cent genetically descendants of the Romans. It is, after all, much more likely that they are as closely related genetically to their Ukrainian, Serbian, Bulgarian and Hungarian neighbours, with whom they have been mixing for centuries, as they are to the Spanish and Portuguese.

There is, then, no inherent or necessary link between language and race. It remains true, however, that in many cases language may be an important or even essential concomitant of ethnic-group membership. This is a social fact, though, and it is important to be clear about what sort of processes may be involved. In some cases, for example, and particularly where languages rather than varieties of a language are involved, linguistic characteristics may be the most important *defining* criteria for ethnic-group membership. For instance, it is less accurate to say that Greeks speak Greek than to state that people who are native speakers of Greek (i.e. who have Greek as their mother tongue) are generally considered to be Greek (at least by other Greeks) whatever their actual nationality. In other cases, particularly where different varieties of the same language are concerned, the connection between language and ethnic group may be a simple one of habitual association, reinforced by social barriers between the groups, where language is an important *identifying* characteristic. By no means all American Blacks speak 'black English', but the overwhelming majority of those who do speak it *are* Blacks, and can be identified as such from their speech alone. In these cases the connection, although not inevitable, is something members of the speech community come to expect, and the breaking of the connection may at first appear to result in incongruity: for this reason many people find it amusing to hear a white person with a West Indian accent. In any case, ethnic-group differentiation in a mixed community is a particular type of social differentiation and, as such, will often have linguistic differentiation associated with it.

Cases of the first type, where language is a *defining* characteristic of ethnic-group membership, are very common on a world scale. Situations of this type are very usual in multilingual Africa, for example. In one suburb outside Accra in Ghana there are native speakers of more than eighty different languages, including such major languages as Twi, Hausa, Ewe and Kru. In most cases, individuals will identify themselves as belonging to a particular ethnic group or tribe on the basis of which of these many languages is their mother tongue (although the majority of the inhabitants are bi- or tri-lingual). The different ethnic groups therefore maintain their separateness and identity as much through language as anything else. This is not only an African phenomenon, of course. The two main ethnic groups in Canada, for example, are distinguished mainly by language. For the most part, it is true, they also have different religions, different histories, cultures and traditions, but the most important defining characteristic is whether they are native speakers of English or French.

In cases of the second type – and these are in many ways more interesting – the separate identity of ethnic groups is signalled, not by different languages, but by different varieties of the same language. Differences of this type may originate in or at least be perpetuated by the same sorts of mechanisms as are involved in the maintenance of social-class dialects: we can suppose that ethnic group differentiation acts as a barrier to the communication of linguistic features in the same way as other social barriers. In the case of ethnic groups, moreover, attitudinal factors are likely to be of considerable importance. Individuals are much more likely to be aware of the fact that they are 'Jewish' or to consider themselves 'Black' than they are to recognize that they are, say, 'lower middle class'. This means that ethnic-group membership may be an important social fact for them. Since, moreover, linguistic differences may be recognized, either consciously or subconsciously, as characteristic of such groups, these differences may be very persistent.

It should also be pointed out that, just as languages are social constructs (see Chapters 1 and 7), so ethnic groups are also relatively fluid entities whose boundaries can change and which can come into being and/or disappear during the course of history. An interesting if distressing example of this comes from Yugoslavia. Between 1918 and the 1990s, Yugoslavia was a multi-ethnic, multilingual nation-state. Most of the country was covered by a geographical dialect continuum (see Chapter 1) of South Slavic dialects. (This continuum also includes the Bulgarian dialects of Bulgaria and neighbouring areas.) Everybody was agreed that the dialects of Slovenia in the north-west were heteronomous to Standard Slovenian. And from 1945, the official position was that the dialects of Yugoslavian Macedonia, in the south, were dialects of Standard Macedonian. In the centre of the country, however – Croatia, Montenegro, Bosnia-Hercegovina and Serbia – the situation was rather more complex. The official position was that the language of these areas was Serbo–Croat (see also Chapter 7).

However, as the name suggests, Serbo-Croat came in two rather different forms: Serbian, which was often written in the Cyrillic alphabet (also used for Bulgarian, Macedonian, Ukrainian and Russian), and was based for the most part (here I am simplifying somewhat) on dialects from the eastern part of central Yugoslavia; and Croatian, which was written in the Latin alphabet, and was based more on western dialects. At various times in history, and by different people, Serbian and Croatian have variously been considered a single language with two different norms, or two different (though mutually intelligible) languages, depending on the prevailing ideology and political situation. Croatian was associated with the Croatian ethnic group, who were dominant in the western area and were traditionally Roman Catholic Christians, and Serbian was associated with the Serbian ethnic group, who were dominant in the eastern part of the area and were traditionally Orthodox Christians. Croats who were natives of Croatia therefore had a choice: they could say that they were native speakers either of Serbo-Croat or of Croatian. Serbs who had grown up in Croatia, on the other hand, and who spoke in exactly the same way, would prefer to say that they spoke Serbo-Croat. The same would apply in reverse to Serbs and Croats living in Serbia.

In Bosnia, the central part of Yugoslavia, the position was even more complex. The dialects spoken in this central part of the dialect continuum are intermediate between those of Croatia and Serbia. There was therefore no particular reason to say that these dialects were dialects of Croatian or dialects of Serbian. Inhabitants of, say, Sarajevo, the capital of Bosnia, might perhaps *say* that they spoke Croatian if they were Croats and a Croat ethnic identity was important to them; similarly, some Serbian Sarajevans might say that they spoke Serbian. In actual fact, however, the dialects they spoke were exactly the same, and therefore the combined name Serbo-Croat actually made much more sense. Using the term Serbo-Croat also seemed more sensible to the other major ethnic group in Bosnia – the Moslems – who, not being either Serbs or Croats, had no reason to favour one language designation over another. This term was also favoured by the large numbers of Yugoslavs who were of ethnically mixed parentage and/or who had come to feel that their national identity as Yugoslavs was what counted for them rather than any particular ethnic identity.

Since the early 1990s, with the break-up of Yugoslavia, this situation has now changed once again. The government of independent Croatia in Zagreb calls its national language Croatian, and strongly favours the Latin alphabet. The Serbian government in Belgrade calls its national language Serbian, and strongly favours the Cyrillic alphabet. In both cases, moreover, governments have attempted to carry out what some opponents have called 'lexical cleansing' – in parallel with the tragic instances of ethnic cleansing (the killing or forcible removal of members of one ethnic group by another) that have occurred in various places in former Yugoslavia. In order to stress the autonomy (see Chapter 1) of Croatian *vis-à-vis* Serbian, and vice versa, words which are thought to be more typical of the other variety are discouraged and are disappearing from newspapers, schoolbooks and so on. Both governments are also attempting to remove words of Turkish origin from their languages, while the Bosnian government is favouring them.

If there is, then, no longer any such language as Serbo-Croat, what are the Moslems of Bosnia to think of themselves as speaking and writing? They would obviously not want to have to choose between the labels 'Serbian' and 'Croatian'. It is therefore not at all surprising that the Bosnian ambassador to the USA has requested that the language of his government should be referred to as *Bosnian*. As we saw in Chapter 1, and as we shall see again in Chapter 7, whether a linguistic variety is a language or not is by no means entirely a linguistic question. When issues of this type are also connected with issues of ethnicity, they can become very complex indeed: one language can end up being three.

For the most part, then, the new governments of former Yugoslavia are attempting to stress their separate nationhoods and ethnicities by focusing on lexical differences.

In other cases, however, ethnic-group differences may be correlated with phonological or grammatical features, as well as or instead of with lexical differences. One of the interesting facts to emerge from Labov's New York study, for example, was that there were slight but apparently significant differences in the English pronunciation of speakers from Jewish and Italian backgrounds. These differences are statistical tendencies rather than clear-cut, reliable signals of ethnic-group differences, but they are clearly due to the fact that the different races tend to form separate groups within the city.

In origin they appear to be due, at least to a certain extent, to the continuing effect of what are often called substratum varieties – the languages or varieties spoken by these groups or their forbears *before* they became speakers of New York City English – Yiddish and Italian. The interference of the old language on the new (a 'Yiddish accent' in English, say) in the first generation seems to have led to hypercorrection of foreign features by the second generation. For example, one of the characteristics of New York English, as we saw in the previous chapter (p. 37), has been the development of high *beard*-like vowels in words of the type *bad, bag*. It seems that this development has been accelerated by the desire, presumably subconscious, of second-generation Italians to avoid speaking English with an Italian accent. Native speakers of Italian tend to use an [a]-type vowel, more open than the English sound, in English words of this type, and their children, in wishing to avoid this pronunciation, may have selected the highest variants of this vowel available to them, i.e. the ones most unlike the typically Italian vowel. Certainly, Italians now show a notably greater tendency to use the higher vowels than do Jews, and this may eventually lead to a situation where high vowels in *bad, bag* become a symbol of identification for New Yorkers from Italian backgrounds. Jewish speakers, on the other hand, tend to have higher vowels than Italians in words of the type *off, lost, dog*, and a similar pattern of hypercorrection may be responsible for this: many native Yiddish speakers who have learnt English as a foreign language do not distinguish the /ɔ/ in *coffee* from the /ʌ/ in *cup*, so that *coffee cup* may be /kɔfɪ kɔp/. Second-generation speakers may therefore have exaggerated the difference between the two vowels, in order to stress the fact that they do make the distinction, with the result that higher vowels occur in *coffee, dog* [dʊəg]. These high vowels are not the *result* of pressures of this sort, since high vowels are by no means confined to Jewish speakers, but they may well have been encouraged by this ethnic-group substratum effect.

A similar kind of substratum effect can be found in the

English of Scotland. Most Scots today tend to think of themselves as simply 'Scottish', but historically speaking they represent descendants of two distinct ethnic groups. To simplify things somewhat, we can say that Highland Scots, whose ancestors came originally from Ireland, were Gaels, and spoke the Celtic language Gaelic (as many of them still do in the West Highlands and on the islands of the Hebrides), while Lowland Scots, who were of Anglo-Saxon descent, were English speakers. Now that English is spoken by nearly everyone in Scotland, this difference still survives in the type of English one can hear in different parts of the country. Lowland Scots speak either a local dialect or Standard English with a local accent (or something in between). Highlanders, on the other hand, speak either standard Scots English (which the group as a whole initially learnt as a foreign language) or something not too far removed from this – not nearly so far from it as the Lowland dialects, in any case. Highlanders do not normally say *I dinna ken*, for example, as Lowlanders might, but rather *I don't know*. There is often, however, a certain amount of substratum influence from Gaelic in the English spoken by Highlanders which may identify them as coming from the Highlands. Native speakers of Gaelic, of course, will often have a Gaelic accent in English, but one can detect lexical and grammatical differences even in the speech of Highlanders who have never spoken Gaelic in their lives. Examples include differences such as the following:

West Highland English	Standard Scots English
Take that whisky here.	*Bring that whisky here.*
I'm seeing you!	*I can see you!*
It's not that that I'm wanting.	*I don't want that.*

In the English-speaking world as a whole one of the most striking examples of linguistic ethnic-group differentiation – and one where the postulated role of some kind of substratum effect is a controversial subject – is the difference we have already noted between the speech of black and white Americans. These differences are by no means manifest in the speech of all Americans, but they are sufficiently widespread to be of considerable interest and importance. It was recognized a long time ago that black Americans spoke English differently from the Whites. A British visitor writing in 1746 said of the American colonists, 'One thing they are very faulty in, with regard to their children . . . is that when young, they suffer them too much to prowl among the young Blacks, which insensibly causes them to imbibe their manners and broken speech.' Differences, then, were noted, and were generally held to be the result of inherent mental or physical differences between the two ethnic groups. Since the English which black people spoke was felt, as the above quotation shows, to be debased or corrupt, the difference was also considered to be the result – and indeed proof – of the inherent inferiority of black people (a fashionable belief at the time). Blacks, it was thought, could not 'speak English properly' since they were simply not capable of it. This view obviously has absolutely no basis in fact, but it cannot be altogether ignored, even today: it was at one time so widely held that it has affected the history of the study of black American English. Many developments in this field have to be viewed against this historical background, and the subject as a whole is in any case fraught with various social and political implications.

The influence of this earlier view lingered on in the following way: since differences in black speech had formerly been ascribed to racial inferiority, the recognition that there was in fact *no* inferiority seemed to imply to linguists who might have thought of studying black English that black speech was not (and could not be) different. This meant that no one could study black speech as such without appearing to be racist, and the subject was therefore neglected for many years. Eventually, however, linguists realized that this attitude was the ethnic-group counterpart to the view, recognized as false, that differences between *social* dialects implied linguistic superiority of one variety over another. If Blacks and Whites spoke differently, this simply meant that there were different (linguistically equally good) ethnic-group language varieties.

Today, therefore, linguists are agreed that there are differences between black speech and white speech and, since there is no way in which one variety can be linguistically superior to another, that it is not racist to say so. The political and social climate is now such that this linguistic problem can be extensively studied and discussed. In fact, such a store of interesting data has been uncovered in the past several years that the study of African American Vernacular English (AAVE) is now one of the major preoccupations of many American linguists. This term is generally used to refer to the nonstandard English spoken by lower-class Blacks (African Americans) in the urban ghettoes of the northern USA and elsewhere. The term *Black English*, as AAVE was sometimes known, had the disadvantage that it suggested that all Blacks speak this one variety of English – which is not the case. The use of the term 'Vernacular', on the other hand, distinguishes those Blacks who do not speak standard American English from those who do, although it still suggests that only one nonstandard variety, homogeneous throughout the whole of the USA, is involved, which is hardly likely, in spite of a surprising degree of similarity between geographically separated varieties. Some of the more typical grammatical characteristics of AAVE are exemplified in the following passages:

TWELVE-YEAR-OLD BOY, DETROIT: 'Sometimes we think she's absolutely crazy. She come in the classroom she be nice and happy . . . the next minute she be hollering at us for no reason, she never have a smile, she'd be giving us a lecture on something that happened twenty years ago.' (From the survey of Detroit speech led by Roger Shuy.)

FIFTEEN-YEAR-OLD HARLEM BOY: 'You know, like some people say if you're good your spirit goin' t'heaven . . .'n' if you bad, your spirit goin' to hell. Well, bullshit! Your spirit goin' to hell anyway. I'll tell you why. 'Cause, you see, doesn' nobody really know that it's a God. An' when they be sayin' if you good, you goin' t'heaven, tha's bullshit, 'cause you ain't goin' to no heaven, 'cause it ain't no heaven for you to go to.' (From a survey of New York speech led by William Labov.)

In any case, although AAVE is now recognized in academic linguistic circles as a normal, valid and interesting variety (or varieties) of English, controversy still remains. While it is recognized that there are differences between AAVE and other varieties, there is disagreement as to the nature of these differences and, in particular, as to their origin. One view is that all features which are said to be characteristic of AAVE can also be found in white speech, although not necessarily in the same combination, and particularly in the white speech of the southern states of the USA. Most features of AAVE, this view claims, are therefore derived historically from British-Isles or other white dialects. They have come to be interpreted as 'black English' because black people have emigrated from the south to the northern cities of the USA, so that what were originally geographical differences have now become, in the north, ethnic-group differences. Furthermore, it is also possible that racial segregation and the growth of ghettoes, which have meant that there has been only minimal contact between Blacks and Whites, have led to the independent development of the English of the two groups – that the two varieties have generated their own distinct linguistic innovations.

The other view claims that many, at least, of the characteristics of AAVE can be explained by supposing that the first American Blacks spoke some kind of English Creole. (I shall leave a full discussion of creole languages until Chapter 8, pp. 160–73. Simply put, however, the term *creole* is applied to a pidgin language which has become the native language of a speech community, and has therefore become expanded again, and acquired all the functions and characteristics of a full natural language. A pidgin is a reduced, simplified, often mixed language evolved for, say, trading purposes by speakers with no common language. Varieties of English Creole (that is, creolized Pidgin English) are widely spoken in the West Indies by people of African descent. In their 'purest' form they are not immediately comprehensible to English speakers, although the vocabulary is similar, and they show fairly considerable influence from African languages.) The hypothesis is, then, that AAVE is not derived from British English dialects, but rather from an English Creole much like that of, say, Jamaica. This view would hold that the earliest American Blacks had a creole as their native language, and that this has, over the years, through a process of *decreolization* (see Chapter 8), come to resemble more and more closely the language of the Whites. In other words, while the language of American Blacks should clearly now be referred to as *English*, those points at which AAVE differs from other English varieties are the result of continuing creole influence. Adherents of this view also suggest that similarities between the speech of Blacks and southern Whites may be due to the influence of the former on the latter, rather than vice versa. There are some clear cases of lexical items which have been introduced into American English from African languages, e.g. *voodoo, pinto* 'coffin', *goober* 'peanut'. It is also probable that *OK* is of West African origin, together with many other words such as *jazz, juke, gig* and *hep*. It is a commentary on the relative status of African Americans that such words are usually described in dictionaries as being of 'unknown origin'.

Let us attempt a short review of the evidence. We shall select some of the most frequently cited characteristics of AAVE, beginning with certain phonological features, and then see how they can best be explained.

1. Many black speakers do not have non-prevocalic /r/ in *cart* or *car*. This feature can quite clearly be traced back to British dialects, and it is also, of course, a feature found in the speech of many American Whites. Many lower-class Blacks, however, also demonstrate loss of intervocalic /r/ (that is, /r/ between vowels) in words like *Carol* and *Paris* (*Ca'ol, Pa'is*), so that *Paris* and *pass, parrot* and *pat* may be homophonous (i.e., sound the same). This feature, though not nearly so commonly, can be heard in the speech of certain southern Whites (British readers will perhaps be familiar with this sort of pronunciation from Westerns: *Howdy she'iff!*), and there are also speakers of British RP who can be heard, for example, to say *very* and similar words

with no /r/: *ve'y nice*. Some black speakers also show loss of /r/ after initial consonants, in certain cases, e.g. *f'om = from*, *p'otect = protect*. This last may be peculiar to AAVE.

2. Many black speakers often do not have /θ/, as in *thing*, or /ð/, as in *that*. In initial position they may be merged with /t/ (rarely) and /d/ respectively, so that *this* is *dis*, for example. This feature is also found, to a certain extent, in the speech of white Americans, but not, it appears, nearly so frequently. It is worth noting that it is also a feature of Caribbean creoles. In other positions, /θ/ and /ð/ may be merged with /f/ and /v/, so that pronunciations such as *b'uvvuh* /bəvə/, for 'brother', may occur. This feature is well-known in London speech.

3. All English speakers, in their normal speech, simplify final consonant clusters in words like *lost, west, desk, end* or *cold* (where both consonants are either voiceless or voiced) where another consonant follows: *los' time, wes' coast*. Where a vowel follows, however, simplification does not occur: *lost elephant, west end*. In AAVE, on the other hand, simplification can take place in all environments, so that pronunciations like *los' elephant, wes' en'* may occur. This means that, in AAVE, plurals of nouns ending in Standard English in *-st, -sp* and *-sk* are often formed on the pattern of *class: classes* rather than of *clasp: clasps*. For example, the plural of *desk* may be *desses*, the plural of *test, tesses*. Consonant-cluster reduction of this type is also a feature of Caribbean creoles, but it appears, too, to be common in the speech of Whites in some parts of the South. However, there also seems to be at least one respect in which some types of AAVE are unique. While some Whites say *tes'* and others *test*, they all have forms like *tester* and *testing*: where the cluster is followed by a suffix beginning with a vowel, simplification does not take place. This is also usual with black speakers, particularly in the North, but there are some African Americans, particularly southern children, who have *tessing* and *tesser*. In other words, the form of items of this type must be assumed to be *tess* for these speakers since they never have a *t* in any

context. We can say, then, that there are some AAVE speakers who, like creole speakers, do not have final consonant clusters of the type *-st*.

4. A number of other features are characteristic of AAVE pronunciation. They include the nasalization of vowels before nasal consonants and the subsequent loss of the consonant: *run, rum, rung* = [rə̃]; vocalization and loss of non-prevocalic /l/: *told* may be pronounced identically with *toe*; and devoicing of final /b/, /d/, /g/ (*bud* and *but* may be distinguished only by the slightly longer vowel of the former) and possible loss of final /d/: *toad* may be pronounced identically with *toe*. All these features, with the possible exception of the last, can be found in various white varieties of English.

Perhaps more central to this argument about the origin of differences between AAVE and other forms of English are grammatical differences.

1. Many black speakers do not have *-s* in third-person singular present-tense forms, so that forms such as *he go, it come, she like* are usual. We saw in Chapter 2, however, that this is also a feature of certain British dialects (it is widespread in East Anglia), and also occurs in the speech of many (particularly southern) white Americans. A certain amount of research, however, has nevertheless suggested that we cannot necessarily ascribe this AAVE feature to an origin in white speech. It has been shown that, in Mississippi, there is a significant difference between the speech of black and white children from the lowest social-class groups with respect to this feature. All the white children studied used some *-s* in the appropriate verb forms, and the average score for the group as a whole was 85 per cent *-s* usage. On the other hand, only 76 per cent of the black children used any *-s*, and the overall average score for *-s* usage was only 13 per cent. There are two possible interpretations of these figures. One interpretation is that both varieties are inherently variable with respect to *-s*, and that – as we have seen to be the case with class dialects – it is simply the proportions of *-s* usage that are different. A second interpretation is that, leaving aside the variety spoken

by the white children, the black children speak a variety of English which, like English Creoles, has no *-s*. The few cases where black children do use the Standard English form (13 per cent), this interpretation would hold, are the result of dialect mixture – the influence of Standard English. Even this second interpretation, however, does not necessarily indicate a creole origin for AAVE – we saw in Chapter 2 that LWC Norwich speakers too are almost invariable in the use of forms without *-s*.

2. An important grammatical characteristic of AAVE is the absence of the copula – the verb *to be* – in the present tense. This characteristic is central to the present controversy. In AAVE, as in Russian, Hungarian, Thai and many other languages including, crucially, creoles, the following type of sentence is grammatical:

> *She real nice.*
> *They out there.*
> *He not American.*
> *If you good, you going to heaven.*

(Where the copula appears in 'exposed' position, as in *I know what it is*, or *Is she?*, it is always present.) What is the origin of this feature in AAVE? Dialectologists point out that in some varieties of white English copula absence is also grammatical. Creolists, on the other hand, point out that the English Creoles of the Caribbean have invariable copula absence. The creolists' case appears to be strong. The same Mississippi study we discussed above, for example, shows that copula deletion in white southern speech, although it does occur, is hardly of the same order as this phenomenon in black speech. While black children deleted *is* in nearly 28 per cent of cases, white children lacked *is* less than 2 per cent of the time. Similarly, African Americans deleted *are* in 77 per cent of cases, while Whites showed deletion in only 21 per cent of cases. Advocates of the creole origin of copula deletion in AAVE can therefore point to the fact (a) that copula deletion does not occur in British dialects, (b) that copula absence is a feature of English-based creoles spoken by Blacks in the Caribbean and (c) that it is much more common in the speech of American Blacks than American Whites. They might also like to suggest that copula deletion in white American – but not British – English is the result of influence from AAVE. Opponents of this view, on the other hand, can point to another crucial problem: is copula deletion in AAVE a grammatical or a phonological phenomenon? Is the copula, that is, 'not there' in AAVE, or is it 'there' but not pronounced? AAVE, as we have seen, is frequently characterized by absence of non-prevocalic /r/. Is, therefore, the deletion of *are* simply an example of this same phenomenon – is *they're* > *they* an example of the same phenomenon as *car* > *cah*? A further point to bear in mind is that, as other linguists have pointed out, AAVE deletes the copula only in those contexts where standard English contracts it – where *is* becomes *'s* or *are* becomes *'re*. It is therefore possible to conclude that copula deletion may be a phonological innovation of AAVE which continues the older process of deletion, thus: *he is* > *he's* > *he*; *they are* > *they're* > *they*.

3. Perhaps the most important characteristic of AAVE is the so-called 'invariant *be*': the use of the form *be* as a finite verb form. For example,

> *He usually be around.*
> *Sometime she be fighting.*
> *Sometime when they do it, most of the problems always be*
>   *wrong.*
> *She be nice and happy.*
> *They sometimes be incomplete.*

At first sight, this use of *be* appears to be no different from its occurrence in certain British dialects, where *I be, he be* etc. correspond to Standard English *I am, he is*. There is, however, a crucial difference between AAVE and all other varieties of English. As the adverbs *usually* and *sometimes* in the above sentences show, invariant *be* is used in AAVE only to indicate 'habitual aspect' – it is only used to refer to some event that is repeated and is not continuous. There is therefore a verbal contrast in AAVE which is not possible in Standard English.

AAVE	Standard English
He busy right now.	*He's busy right now.*
Sometime he be busy.	*Sometimes he's busy.*

In Standard English the verb form is the same in both cases, whereas they are distinct in AAVE because, while the first sentence does not refer to some repeated non-continuous action, the second does. In AAVE, constructions such as *He be busy right now* and *He be my father* are not grammatical sentences. (The latter would imply, 'He is only my father from time to time.') This kind of distinction in the verb is certainly reminiscent of creole languages. In Caribbean creoles, verb aspect – the distribution of an event through time (whether it is repeated, continuous, completed, and so on) – tends to be of greater importance than tense – the actual location of an event in time (see p. 169). At the same time, it should be said that this sort of habitual–non-habitual distinction is not unknown in British-Isles dialects, although where it does occur it does so in by no means exactly the same form. In the old-fashioned dialect of Dorset, for example, *He beat her*, meaning 'He beat her on one particular occasion in the past,' contrasts with *He did beat her*, meaning that he was in the habit of doing so. There are, however, two other respects in which the aspectual system of AAVE differs from that of Standard English (and more closely resembles that of some creoles). AAVE and Standard English have in common a present perfect verb form, *I have talked*, and past perfect form, *I had talked*. But AAVE has, in addition, two further forms: *I done talked*, which has been called 'completive aspect', indicating that the action is completed; and *I been talked*, the 'remote aspect', indicating an event that occurred in the remote past. Completive aspect can be found in certain white dialects, but the remote aspect appears to be peculiar to AAVE (although it is not, it must be said, particularly common even there).

4. Three final grammatical characteristics of AAVE worthy of mention are: AAVE question inversion, 'existential *it*', and 'negativized auxiliary pre-position'. Rules for question

inversion in indirect questions in AAVE differ from those in Standard English, and result in sentences such as *I asked Mary where did she go* and *I want to know did he come last night*. Existential *it* occurs where Standard English has *there*. For example, *It's a boy in my class name Joey; It ain't no heaven for you to go to; Doesn't nobody know that it's a God*. This last sentence also illustrates negativized auxiliary preposition. In AAVE, if a sentence has a negative indefinite like *nobody, nothing*, then the negative auxiliary (*doesn't, can't*) can be placed at the beginning of the sentence: *Can't nobody do nothing about it; Wasn't nothing wrong with that* (with statement intonation).

To summarize, there are four possible views one can take with respect to the controversy about the origins of AAVE, depending on which of the views one accepts on its origins, and what one considers the present-day situation to be.

1. The 'different-equals-inferior' view maintains that there are no differences between the speech of black and white Americans and that, therefore, all characteristics of AAVE can be traced back to British dialects or are American innovations that also occur in white speech in the USA. Linguists would not now accept this view, since it has been demonstrated to their satisfaction that there are some significant differences. The view still has its adherents outside linguistics, however. Because of the legacy of the 'different-equals-inferior' position, some black people still feel that the academic discussion of AAVE is an attempt to discriminate against them, and would prefer that the subject not be discussed. This is not altogether surprising in view of the prejudices many people still have about language, and it is noteworthy that even militant African American leaders, while content to use 'black slang' as an in-group language, have made no reference to AAVE as, say, a dialect to be proud of. As recently as 1949, one writer claimed that Blacks 'could not pronounce r' because of their 'thick lips'. (He was presumably referring to the lack in AAVE, as in RP, of non-prevocalic /r/. How Blacks are able to articulate prevocalic /r/ he does

not explain.) This view is clearly absurd, but it still colours people's attitudes to this subject.

2. The 'dialectologist' view recognizes that there are differences between AAVE and white speech but claims, nevertheless, that AAVE is historically derived from British dialects. This view has been popular with some American dialectologists, who suggest that the differences are due to a different *combination* of British dialect features; to the fact that AAVE may have preserved certain archaic features now lost in other varieties; and to later, independent developments in the different varieties. They point out that it would be surprising, in view of the cultural division in America between Whites and Blacks, if their speech had not developed differently. They suggest, in particular, that the development of the urban ghetto and of barriers to communication imposed by poverty and deprivation has been instrumental in the development of differences. Characteristics of white and black speech were originally the same, but have been 'skewed' by the colour-caste system. (This is one way of explaining the different proportions of -*s* usage in verbs in the two ethnic groups.) Against this view it has been pointed out that many of the characteristics said to be typical of ghetto speech can also be found in southern rural black speech.

3. The 'integrationist' view claims that, although historical records provide a certain amount of evidence to suggest that Blacks in America used to speak an African-influenced creole type of English, there are no longer any features of AAVE which cannot be found in white speech. In other words, although there was formerly a difference, AAVE and some types of southern white speech are now indistinguishable. This, it could be claimed, is due to the gradual convergence of creole English with English, and also to some influence of AAVE on white speech. This view does not appear to have much support amongst linguists, but it will be obvious that the stressing of present-day similarities between black and white speech may find support from those who favour an 'integrationist' approach to America's racial problems.

4. The 'creolist' view maintains that there are (as most

linguists are now agreed) significant differences between AAVE and other varieties, and that these can be best explained in terms of the creole origins of AAVE. AAVE, that is, is an English Creole like those spoken in the Caribbean which has gradually become more and more decreolized. One piece of evidence that may support this view has been based on a particular feature of AAVE syntax. In Standard English and white varieties of nonstandard English the following sentence types can occur:

> Standard English: *We were eating – and drinking too.*
> White nonstandard: *We was eatin' – and drinkin' too.*

In these varieties it would be possible for a fuller form to occur: *We were eating – and we were drinking too*, but it is more normal to omit the pronoun *we* and the auxiliary *were/was* in the second clause. In many English Creoles, on the other hand, it is more usual to omit only the auxiliary. Consider the following translations of the above example into Gullah, an English Creole spoken in an isolated part of the coastal American South, Jamaican Creole and Sranan, an English Creole spoken in Surinam:

> Gullah: *We bin duh nyam – en' we duh drink, too.*
> Jamaican C: *We ben a nyam – an' we a drink, too.*
> Sranan: *We ben de nyang – en' we de dringie, too.*

(In this example *nyam* and *nyang* = *eat*, *bin* is the past tense marker or auxiliary – note the parallel with AAVE *I been talked* – and *duh*, *a* and *de* are continuous aspect markers corresponding to English *-ing* forms.) Strikingly enough, the AAVE form, although superficially more like the Standard English and nonstandard white English forms, is in fact basically more like the Creole examples in that it usually omits only the auxiliary:

> AAVE: *We was eatin' – an' we drinkin', too.*

My own view is that, even if many of the features of AAVE can be found in various white dialects, AAVE itself functions today as a separate ethnic-group variety which identifies its speakers as being black rather than white. Many of the features of AAVE must be ascribed to the fact that the first Blacks in the United States spoke some kind of English Creole – the resemblances between AAVE and West Indian creoles are at some points too striking to ignore. This, however, does not necessarily indicate that other features of AAVE may not be traceable directly to British dialects. In a few cases, for instance, archaisms lost in white speech may be preserved in AAVE. In other cases, the controversy about the origins of AAVE may be rather meaningless. Verb forms like *he love, she do* can probably be explained as the result of creole background *and* British dialect influence, the one reinforcing the other. And it is worth remembering, too, that English Creoles themselves are historically also derived partly from British dialects.

More recently, echoes of the 'skewing' view have appeared in the work of American sociolinguists prominent in the study of AAVE. Some research appears to suggest that, even if AAVE is descended from an English-based Creole which has, over the centuries, come to resemble more and more closely the English spoken by other Americans, this process has now begun to swing into reverse. This 'divergence hypothesis' states that, because of a lack of integration between black and white communities, particularly in urban areas, AAVE and white dialects of English are now once more beginning to grow apart. In other words, changes are taking place in white dialects which are not occurring in AAVE, and vice versa. Quite naturally, this hypothesis has aroused considerable attention in the United States because, if true, it provides a dramatic reflection of the racially divided nature of American society.

At the moment, American linguists are not agreed as to exactly what is happening. However, it has been shown that sound changes that are occurring in the vowel systems of white speakers in, for example, Philadelphia – such as the raising of vowels in words like *write* and *type* to [əi], e.g. [rəit] – are not occurring in the English of black speakers in the same city. On the other hand, AAVE appears to be undergoing some grammatical changes which are not affecting white dialects at all. For example, usage of future resultative *be done* appears to be a new and increasingly common grammatical device in the speech of younger AAVE speakers, as in this example observed in Los Angeles by the African American sociolinguist John Baugh: *I'll be done killed that motherfucker if he tries to lay a hand on my kid again.*

4. Language and Sex

So far in the book we have been discussing some of the relationships to be found in linguistic communities between social differentiation and linguistic differentiation, together with some of the forms this linguistic differentiation can take. The two main types of social differentiation we have dealt with so far have been social stratification and ethnic-group differentiation. In both these cases we were able to point to parallels between social differentiation and geographical differentiation with respect to their effects on language: social distance, it appears, has the same kind of linguistic consequences as geographical distance. Ethnic and social-class groups, like regional groups, have linguistic characteristics in common because their members communicate more frequently with each other than with outsiders.

In this chapter, we shall be dealing with an aspect of linguistic differentiation that does not appear to be susceptible to the same kind of explanation. It is known from linguistic research that in many societies the speech of men and women differs. In some cases the differences are quite small and are not generally noticed: they are probably taken for granted in the same way as, say, different gestures or facial expressions. For example, in many accents of American English it has been found that women's vowels are more peripheral (more front, more back, higher, or lower) than men's. In other cases the differences may be quite large, overtly noted, and perhaps even actively taught to young children. In Gros Ventre, for example, an American Indian language from the north-eastern USA, palatalized dental stops in men's speech correspond to palatalized velar stops in the speech of women – men:

/djatsa/; women: /kjatsa/ 'bread'. Again, in Yukaghir, a northeast Asian language, /tj/ and /dj/ in male speech correspond to /ts/ and /dz/ in the speech of women. We can be fairly sure in this last case that these differences are consciously made, since they also correlate with *age* differences: children also use the female /ts/ and /dz/ forms, while old people of both sexes use yet another set of variants, /čj/, /ǰj/. This means that a male speaker uses three different forms in the course of his lifetime, and is presumably therefore aware of the two changeovers that he makes.

Generally speaking, we cannot explain differences of this kind in terms of social distance. In most societies men and women communicate freely with one another, and there appear to be few social barriers likely to influence the density of communication between the sexes. We cannot, therefore, account for the development of gender differences in language in the same way as class, ethnic-group, or geographical dialects. How, then, *do* such differences arise? Why do men and women often speak differently? Let us take a few examples of the kind of differences that have been reported, and attempt to see what factors may have been important in their development. We begin with some of the larger, overtly recognized differences.

The classic example of linguistic sex differentiation, well known to students of language, comes from the West Indies. It was often reported that when Europeans first arrived in the Lesser Antilles and made contact with the Carib Indians who lived there, they discovered that the men and women 'spoke different languages'. This would of course have been a very startling discovery, and one that does not appear to have been paralleled anywhere else in the world: nowhere else has sex differentiation been found to be so great that people have been led to propose that there were actually distinct men's and women's languages. However, it does seem that these reports (or later embellishments of them) were stretching things somewhat. A contemporary report (from the seventeenth century) says:

The men have a great many expressions peculiar to them, which the women understand but never pronounce themselves. On the other hand the women have words and phrases which the men never use, or they would be laughed to scorn. Thus it happens that in their conversations it often seems as if the women had another language than the men.

From the evidence supplied by this seventeenth-century writer, as well as from the above quotation, it seems certain that, although there were clear differences between men's and women's speech, only a relatively small number of vocabulary items were involved. The men and women, that is, did *not* speak different languages. Rather, they spoke different varieties of the same language – the differences were lexical only. Even so, how can we explain these particular differences? The Indians themselves had an explanation which has also been quite widely accepted. The contemporary report quoted above continues:

> The savage natives of Dominica say that the reason for this is that when the Caribs came to occupy the islands these were inhabited by an Arawak tribe which they exterminated completely, with the exception of the women, whom they married in order to populate the country. It is asserted that there is some similarity between the speech of the continental Arawaks and that of the Carib women.

The differences, that is, were believed to be the result of the mixing of the two language groups, Carib and Arawak, divided on sex lines, as the result of an invasion. This may or may not be true, and it is probably unlikely that we shall ever know what the origin of these differences was. One thing is clear, however: even if this explanation is true, we cannot apply it to the origin of linguistic gender differences in other parts of the world. We must also regard the 'invasion' theory, even in this particular case, as rather suspect. First, the reported differences amongst the Carib Indians resemble to a considerable extent those found elsewhere in other American Indian languages. Secondly, the linguist Otto Jespersen has advanced another explanation which is, at least, equally plausible and which will perhaps apply (as we would wish) to other cases as well. Jespersen suggests that sex differentiation, in some cases, may be the result of the phenomenon of *taboo* which we discussed in Chapter 1. He points out that it is known that when Carib men were on the war-path they would use a number of words which only adult males were allowed to employ. If women or uninitiated boys used these words, bad luck was considered likely to result. Taboo may perhaps therefore have a powerful influence on the growth of separate sex vocabularies generally. If taboos become associated with particular objects or activities such that, say, women are not permitted to use the original name, then new words or paraphrases are likely to be used instead, and sex differentiation of vocabulary items will result. Examples of taboo as an explanatory factor come also from other parts of the world. In Zulu, for example, it has been reported that a wife was not allowed to mention the name of her father-in-law or his brothers, and she might be put to death if she broke this taboo. Moreover, we saw in Chapter 1 that taboo can extend to words which simply resemble the original tabooed words. In Zulu, it appears that this process could go so far as to include particular sounds of the language. Say, for example, that the tabooed name contained the sound /z/. This might mean, apparently, that the woman in question would not be able to use a word like *amanzi* 'water' without converting it to a form without the tabooed sound, *amandabi*. If this kind of process became generalized to all the women in the community, then it can be seen that distinct sex dialects might result.

Taboo, however, is not a particularly good explanation of linguistic gender differentiation. First, it is not really clear how differences of the above type could become generalized to the whole community. And secondly, in many other cases it is quite clear that we are not dealing with taboo. In some of these cases the explanation is quite readily apparent. For example, in Chiquito, an American Indian language of Bolivia, if a woman wants to say 'my brother' she says *ičbausi*, whereas a male speaker would say *tsaruki*. This, however, does not constitute a sex difference of the same order as those we have already discussed; rather it is a result of the Chiquito kinship and gender systems. Just as we distinguish in English between the sex of close relations referred to or addressed (*brother, sister, uncle, aunt*), so many other languages also have different terms according to the sex of the speaker doing the referring or addressing. This is simply a recognition of the fact that the relationship brother–sister is different from the relationship brother–brother. Other relationships in Chiquito are differentiated in the same way:

	male speaker	female speaker
my father	*ijai*	*išupu*
my mother	*ipaki*	*ipapa*

This sort of differentiation is similar to that found in the pronominal systems. In English we differentiate between the sexes only in the third-person singular: *he, she*. In French the third-person plural is also differentiated: *ils, elles*, while in Finnish there is no distinction even in the singular: *hän* can be equivalent to either *he* or *she*. In other languages of the world, gender differentiation extends to the second person and even to the first person. In Thai, for example, in polite conversation between equals, a man will say *phom* for the first-person singular pronoun 'I' whereas a woman will refer to herself as *dichan*.

There are other cases where taboo is clearly not a factor, but where the explanation is not so simple as these gender and kinship examples. In research done in the 1930s, for example, quite notable sex differences were found in the American Indian language Koasati, a language of the Muskogean family, spoken in Louisiana. The differences, which seemed to be disappearing at the time the research was carried out, involved the phonological shapes of particular verb forms. Consider the following examples:

	male	female
'He is saying'	/kaːs/	/kãː/
'Don't lift it!'	/lakaučiːs/	/lakaučin/
'He is peeling it'	/mols/	/mol/
'You are building a fire'	/oːsč/	/oːst/

From this list the differences appear to be rather haphazard, but they are in fact entirely predictable according to a series of fairly complicated rules. (For example, if the female form ends in a nasalized vowel, then the male form has a non-nasalized vowel plus /s/, e.g. female /lakauwã:/; male /lakauwa:s/ 'He will lift it.') There is also good reason to believe that the same kind of differentiation formerly existed in other Muskogean languages, but that in these languages the women's varieties have died out. (This is partly confirmed by the fact that in Koasati itself it was only the older women who preserved the distinct forms. Younger women and girls used the male forms.) Differences of this kind have been found in a number of other American languages. In addition to the Gros Ventre case mentioned above, sex differences of some kind have been found in the American Indian languages Yana and Sioux, and in the Inuit (Eskimo) spoken in Baffin Island.

Taboo does not appear to be involved in any of these cases. The two varieties of Koasati, for example, were learnt from parents who were equally familiar with both and would correct children when necessary. If a small boy said /kã:/, for example, his mother would stop him and, herself using the male form, say, 'No, you must say /ka:s/.' No taboo prohibition prevented her from using this form. Similarly, when relating stories a man could quite properly use female forms when quoting a female character – and vice versa. Another example which helps to make this point comes from Darkhat Mongolian. The back rounded vowels /u/ and /o/ in men's speech correspond to the mid vowels /ʉ/ and /ɵ/ in women's speech, whereas male /ʉ/ and /ɵ/ correspond to female /y/ and /ø/ – front vowels. Although female speakers do not use /ʉ/ and /ɵ/ where male speakers use them, there is no taboo prohibition to prevent them from using these sounds in other cases:

Figure 3. Sex differentiation in Darkhat Mongolian

How *can* we explain differences of this type? In Koasati some, at least, of the female forms appeared to be *older* historically than the male forms. In other words, it seemed that linguistic changes had taken place in the male variety which had not been followed through (or were only just beginning to be followed) in the women's speech. The same sort of phenomenon occurs in other languages. Chukchi, for example, is a language spoken in Siberia. In some dialects, the female variety has intervocalic consonants in some words, particularly /n/ and /t/, which are not present in male forms; for example, male: /nitvaqaat/; female: /nitvaqenat/. Loss of intervocalic consonants is a much more frequent and expected sound change than the unmotivated insertion of consonants, and very many examples of loss of consonants in this position have been attested in languages from all parts of the world. This kind of distinction would therefore appear to provide a clear indication that the female variety is older than the male dialect. In more than one language, therefore, women's speech is more conservative than that of men.

Another clue comes, again, from Koasati, and in particular from the attitudes which the Koasati people themselves had to the two varieties. Older speakers, particularly the men, tended to say, when asked, that they thought the women's variety was *better* than that used by men. This is important, because it ties in in an interesting way with data we have from technologically more advanced speech communities. It also shows us that the gender varieties are not simply different: in at least two languages the male varieties are *innovating* and the female *conservative*, and in one case the female variety is evaluated as *better* as opposed to *worse*. Differences of this type should be easier to explain than linguistic differences, pure and simple.

Let us now take this discussion a stage further by examining some sex differences in English, where the differences are generally of the smaller, less obvious and more subconscious type. There are, it is true, a number of words and phrases which tend to be sex-bound. (Most of these, incidentally, seem to be exclamations of some sort. This suggests that taboo may be involved in some way: it is certainly tradition-ally more acceptable in our society for men to swear and use taboo words than it is for women.) Mostly, however, differ-ences within English are phonetic and phonological, and taboo *cannot* be used as an explanation. The differences, moreover, are generally so insignificant that most people are not at all consciously aware of them. It is also important to notice that these differences represent statistical tendencies and not absolute distinctions. Grammatical differences may also be involved, as we shall see below.

Most of the evidence we have for gender differences in English has come from some of the urban dialect surveys carried out in Britain and America that we have already mentioned. The sets of data these surveys have provided have one striking feature in common. In all the cases so far examined, it has been shown that, allowing for other factors such as social class, ethnic group and age, women on average use forms which more closely approach those of the standard variety or the prestige accent than those used by men, al-though we cannot predict which form a given man or woman is going to use on a given occasion. In other words, female speakers of English, like their Koasati counterparts, tend to use linguistic forms which are considered to be 'better' than male forms. In Chapter 2 we examined some of the ways in which linguistic variables are correlated with social class. These variables can also be used in the same sort of way to illustrate gender differentiation.

Consider the following figures. In Detroit, higher-class speakers use fewer instances of non-standard multiple nega-tion (e.g. *I don't want none*) than lower-class speakers. Allow-ing for social class, however, women on average use fewer such forms than men do:

Percentage of multiple negation used

	UMC	LMC	UWC	LWC
Male	6.3	32.4	40.0	90.1
Female	0.0	1.4	35.6	58.9

In the case of the LMC and the LWC these differences are very big indeed: men are much more likely to say *I don't want none* than women are. Women, this suggests, are far more sensitive to the stigmatized nature of this grammatical feature than men. This sensitivity, moreover, is not confined to grammatical features. In the speech of Detroit Blacks, for instance, women use a far higher percentage of non-prevocalic /r/ (a prestige feature here as in New York) than men, allowing for social class:

Percentage of non-prevocalic /r/ in Detroit Black speech

	UMC	LMC	UWC	LWC
Male	66.7	52.5	20.0	25.0
Female	90.0	70.0	44.2	31.7

Some writers have attempted to explain this sort of pattern in the black community by pointing out that the lower-class black ghetto family is typically matriarchal and that it is the mother of a family who conducts business with the outside world and who has job contacts with speakers of prestige varieties. This explanation is not adequate, however, since exactly the same pattern is found in the white community and in British English. In Norwich English, for example, the same sort of pattern emerges with the (ng) variable (whether speakers say *walking* or *walkin'*). The table below gives the percentage of non-RP-*in'* forms used by speakers in different class and sex groups:

	MMC	LMC	UWC	MWC	LWC
Male	4	27	81	91	100
Female	0	3	68	81	97

Once again, women use a higher percentage of 'better' forms than men do. In London English, too, men are more likely than women to use glottal stops in words like *butter* and *but*. And this phenomenon is not confined only to British and American English. In South Africa, for example, research has been carried out in the Transvaal, comparing the speech of English-speaking male and female high-school pupils of the same age in the same town. A study was made of the pronunciation of four vowels:

1. The vowel of *gate*, which in South Africa ranges from high-prestige RP [geɪt] to low-prestige South African [gɜɪ], with a lower and more central first element to the diphthong, as in RP *bird*.

2. The vowel of *can't*, which ranges from RP [kɑːnt] to South African [kɒːnt], with a vowel close in quality to that found in RP *on* – a low back rounded vowel.

3. The vowel of *out*, which ranges from RP [aut] to South African [æut], with a higher front first element resembling the vowel in RP *cat*.

4. The vowel in *boy*, which ranges from RP [bɔɪ] to a variant with a high back rounded first element [buɪ] as in RP *school*.

The results, giving the percentage of boys and girls using each variant in each case, are given below:

	RP		Non-RP	
gate	[geɪt]	[gɜɪt]		
boys	0	100		
girls	62	38		
can't	[kaːnt]	[kɒːnt]		
boys	0	100		
girls	62	38		
out	[aut]	[aut]	[æut]	
boys	25	17	58	
girls	85	15	0	
boy	[bɔɪ]	[bɔɪ]	[boɪ]	[buɪ]
boys	0	16	42	42
girls	15	38	47	0

The boys, we can see, are much more likely than the girls to use nonstandard local pronunciations.

In different parts of the English-speaking world, then, as well as in Koasati, female speakers have been found to use forms considered to be 'better' or more 'correct' than those used by men. A woman interviewed in a Norwegian dialect survey said, when asked why she used the prestige pronunciation [ɛg] 'egg' while her brothers said [æg]: 'It isn't *done* for a woman to say [æg].' In fact, gender differentiation of this type is the single most consistent finding to emerge from sociolinguistic work around the world in the past thirty years. Why should this be? The correct answer is that we do not know, but sociolinguists have come up with a number of different, necessarily speculative suggestions.

Firstly, it has been pointed out that working-class speech, like certain other aspects of working-class culture in our society, seems to have connotations of or associations with masculinity, which may lead men to be more favourably disposed to nonstandard linguistic forms than women. This, in turn, may be because working-class speech is associated with the 'toughness' traditionally supposed to be characteristic of working-class life – and 'toughness' is quite widely considered to be a desirable masculine characteristic.

Secondly, it has also been pointed out that many societies seem to expect a higher level of adherence to social norms – better behaviour – from women than they do from men. If father comes home drunk on Saturday night and vomits over the living-room carpet, this is bad. But if mother does the same, many people would feel it is worse. As the New Zealand sociolinguist Elizabeth Gordon has pointed out, one area where 'better' behaviour is obviously expected from women, because of double standards in our society, is in the area of sexual activity. She suggests that women may have a tendency to speak in a more prestigious way so as not to be thought sexually promiscuous.

Given that there are linguistic variables in a speech community which are involved in co-variation with social class (higher-class forms being more statusful or 'correct' than lower-class forms), then there are social pressures on speakers to acquire prestige or to appear 'correct' by employing the higher-class forms. Other things being equal, however, it is probably true to say that these pressures will tend to be stronger on women. On the other hand, there will also be pressure, as we saw in the case of Martha's Vineyard, to continue using less prestigious nonstandard variants as a signal of group solidarity and personal identity. These pressures, however, will tend to be stronger on men than on women, because of concepts of masculinity current in our society.

It has to be stressed that these explanations are, at the moment, just suggestions. It does seem, however, that gender differentiation in language arises because, as we have already seen, language, as a social phenomenon, is closely related to social attitudes. Men and women are socially different in that society lays down different social roles for them and expects different behaviour patterns from them. Language simply reflects this social fact.

The larger and more inflexible the difference between the social roles of men and women in a particular community, the larger and more rigid the linguistic differences tend to be. Our English examples have all consisted of *tendencies* for women to use more 'correct' forms than men. The examples of *distinct* male and female varieties all came from technologically primitive food-gathering or nomadic communities where sex roles are much more clearly delineated. If the social roles of men and women change, moreover, as they seem to be doing currently in many societies, then it is likely that gender differences in language will change or diminish also, and we shall see some evidence that this may be so below.

As far as English is concerned we have some interesting evidence about the way in which social values and sex roles affect speakers' attitudes towards linguistic variants – and hence their actual usage of these variants. We already have plenty of evidence to show that, in England, Standard English and the RP accent have high prestige. (It is well-known, for example, that speakers who are paying considerable attention to their speech will move linguistically in the direction of these statusful varieties.) What, however, of the argument that working-class speech has favourable connotations for male speakers? Can we actually show that this is the case?

The argument really hinges on the belief that lower-class, nonstandard linguistic varieties also have some kind of 'prestige', and that this is particularly so in the case of men. (We can assume that this is the case: otherwise there would be far more RP and Standard English speakers than there in fact are. But it would be very satisfying to be able to show this.) Labov has called this kind of 'prestige' *covert prestige* because attitudes of this type are not usually overtly expressed, and depart markedly from the mainstream societal values (of schools and other institutions) of which everyone is consciously aware. Favourable words like 'good' and 'nice', for instance, are usually reserved for standard prestige varieties.

One example of the evidence which shows that covert prestige exists is as follows. In the urban dialect survey of Norwich, informants were asked to take part in a 'self-evaluation test', in order to investigate what they *believed* themselves to say as opposed to what they actually did say. In this test, words were read aloud to the informants with two or more different pronunciations. For example:

tune   1. [tjuːn]   2. [tuːn]

(The first variant has a y-glide [j], the second 'toon' does not. Both pronunciations are current in Norwich, the former, being the RP pronunciation, having more prestige than the latter.) Informants were then asked to say, by marking a number on a chart, which of the pronunciations they normally used themselves. By comparing the results of this test with the data actually tape-recorded during the interviews, it became possible to note discrepancies between what informants thought or claimed they said and what they *actually* said. The results for the vowel of *tune, student, music* etc. were very interesting, and are shown in Table 7. Informants are divided into two groups: those who used 50 per cent or more [j] in their tape-recorded conversations were considered to be [j] glide-users, and those with less than 50 per cent non-users. This table shows that a majority of informants were accurate in their self-reporting: 84 per cent of those who did not use [j] glides in conversation stated that they did not do so, and only

Table 7. Self-evaluation of tune *in Norwich*

| | % informants | |
	glide-use claimed	glide-use not claimed
actual glide-users	60	40
actual non-users	16	84

16 per cent of non-users actually claimed to use the more prestigious variant when they did not in fact use it. But notice the glide-users. While 60 per cent of them were accurate in their reporting, as many as 40 per cent of them actually claimed to use the lower-status, *non-prestige* pronunciation [tu:n] even though they *normally* said [tju:n], as demonstrated by the tape-recordings. We can call these people 'under-report-ers' since they claimed to use less statusful variants than they actually used, and the 16 per cent group, who went the other way, 'over-reporters'.

If we now break these scores down by sex, the results are rather revealing. Of the 40 per cent under-reporters, half were men and half women. But of the 16 per cent over-reporters, *all* were women. The figures for the sample as a whole are given in Table 8.

Table 8. Over- and under-reporting of tune *in Norwich*

| | % informants | | |
	total	male	female
over-reporting	13	0	29
under-reporting	7	6	7
accurate	80	94	64

Male informants, we can see, are strikingly more accurate than their female counterparts. The women, we can say, report themselves, in very many cases, as using higher-class variants than they actually do – presumably because they wish they did use them or think they ought to and perhaps, therefore, actually believe that they do. Speakers, that is, report themselves as using the form at which they are aiming and which has favourable connotations for them, rather than the form they actually use. (No *conscious* deceit is involved, it seems.)

Consider, now, the figures in Table 9. This shows the results of the self-evaluation test for the vowel in Norwich English in *ear, here, idea*. (There are two main variants of this vowel in Norwich: 1. [ɪə], as in RP, and 2. [ɛː], with the vowel of *care*, so that *ear* and *air, here* and *hair* are the same.) This table shows not only that a majority of women reported themselves as using RP [ɪə] when in fact they did *not*, but also that as many as *half* the men went the other way and *under*-reported – they reported themselves as using a *less* statusful, more lower-class form than they normally used. This then provides us with evidence to suggest that male Norwich speakers, at a subconscious level, are very favourably disposed to nonstandard, low-status speech forms – so much so, in fact, that they claim to use these forms or hear themselves as using them *even when they do not do so*. A large number of male speakers, it seems, are more concerned with acquiring *covert prestige* than with obtaining social status (as this is more usually defined). For Norwich men (and, we can perhaps assume, for men elsewhere) working-class speech is statusful and prestigious.

Table 9. *Over- and under-reporting of* ear *in Norwich*

| | % informants | | |
	total	male	female
over-reporting	43	22	68
under-reporting	33	50	14
accurate	23	28	18

The clear contrast with the scores of the women informants underlines this point, and demonstrates that they, on the other hand (with as many as 68 per cent over-reporting in the case of *ear*-type vowels), are much more favourably disposed to middle-class, RP forms. These different attitudes on the part of men and women explain why the sex differentiation portrayed in the case of Norwich *ng* and the two Detroit variables takes the form it does. Because society evaluates different characteristics differently in the two sexes, covert prestige exerts a more powerful influence on men, and 'normal' prestige on women. The result is the social-class-linked gender accent differentiation we have seen portrayed above.

In Koasati and, in particular, in Chukchi, we saw that women's speech was more conservative than that of men. Linguistic changes, that is, were led by men, and women followed along later, as it were, if at all. Patterns of a similar kind, albeit of a more complex type, are also found in Western communities: it seems, for example, that women are more conservative than men when it comes to linguistic changes which are operating in the direction away from the prestige standard – glottal stop realizations of /t/ in English, for example. In those cases where there is some kind of high-status variety or national norm, then changes in the direction of this norm appear, on the other hand, to be led more frequently by women. In Hillsboro, North Carolina, for instance, women appear to be in the vanguard of the change from an older prestige norm to a newer one. Whereas educated southern speech of the type formerly considered prestigious in Hillsboro is r-less, women especially are now tending to use the more widespread national prestige norm with non-prevocalic /r/ in words such as *car* and *cart*.

A similar development has taken place in the Larvik area in southern Norway, where forms from the town are spreading out into the countryside and taking over from the lower-status, earlier, rural forms. Here again women are leading the way. In many families it is possible to isolate three different stages: fathers in the country districts will be more conservative than their sons, and their sons in turn will be more conservative than their mothers and sisters. Women, for example, are more likely to use the prestige town form [mɛlk] 'milk' than the more typically rural form [mjæɾk], and on the whole appear to be a generation ahead of male speakers.

In Norwich, too, the same sort of pattern emerges, with women in the vanguard of changes towards prestige pronunciation. There is, however, one exception in Norwich English where a linguistic change has upset the normal pattern of sex differentiation. The variable involved in this unusual case is the vowel of words such as *top*, *hot*, *dog*. In Norwich this can have a low back rounded vowel, as in RP [tɒp], or an unrounded vowel, [tap]. The figures below show the percentage of unrounded non-RP forms used by different speakers:

	MMC	LMC	UWC	MWC	LWC
Male	1	11	44	64	80
Female	0	1	68	71	83

For the two middle-class groups, as one would expect, male scores are higher (they use more non-prestige forms) than female scores. For the three working-class groups, on the other hand, the scores are consistently the other ('wrong') way round: female scores are higher than male scores. We may explain this in the following way: the vowel of *top* is currently undergoing linguistic change in Norwich: rounded vowels of the RP-type are on the increase, as these age-group figures for percentage of unrounded vowels show.

age-group	%
10–29	55
30–49	63
50–69	67
70+	93

The change, however, is taking place in an interesting and unusual way. The newer, rounded vowel is being introduced into Norwich English from RP by middle-class women who are favourably disposed to prestige forms and therefore use nearly 100 per cent of rounded vowels. It is also being introduced, however, by working-class men, in imitation of the working-class speech of the London area and the neighbouring county of Suffolk. These working-class accents, which also use [ɒ], have favourable connotations (covert prestige) for Norwich men, and they therefore use more rounded vowels and have lower scores than working-class women. This, then, is an unusual case of overt prestige and covert prestige coinciding, and it illustrates the role that gender differentiation can play in linguistic change.

Tendencies towards gender-based linguistic differentiation, then, are the result of different social attitudes towards the behaviour of men and women, and of the attitudes men and women themselves consequently have to language as a social symbol. These attitudes, it is perhaps worth noting, may be of particular importance in an educational situation. In the West Indies, for example, it has been found that children begin to acquire sex-bound attitudes towards standard English as early as the age of six or seven. In a study of children who were native speakers of English Creole (see Chapter 8) learning Standard English it was found that, although there were no sex differences in their speech to begin with, after six months of learning, the girls' speech had changed more extensively towards the prestige norm they were being taught than that of the boys – although both had changed to some extent. At the end of the six-month period, for example, boys were using 29 per cent nonstandard verb-phrases, while girls were using only $7\frac{1}{2}$ per cent. It was also noticed that, when they thought they were not being observed, some of the boys enjoyed themselves by mimicking, in girlish voices, some of the standard forms that they had learnt. They associated standard speech with femininity, and their motivation to learn was presumably, therefore, that much weaker than the girls'. (This represents, of course, the other side of the 'covert prestige' coin.)

So far in this chapter we have been discussing sex differences in language in terms of the way things are, and in terms of what people have traditionally felt to be appropriate. However, while we noted above that 'society lays down different roles' for men and women, it is equally true that what society lays down can and does change – and will change if enough members of the society feel that it is desirable that this should happen. In most Western societies, for instance, many people have altered or are altering the way they feel about what is appropriate as far as gender roles are concerned. And these beginnings of a move away from gender-role stereotyping probably explain the fact that linguistic differences between younger men and women – a very interesting finding from sociolinguistic research – are statistically smaller than in the case of older speakers.

Much of this reduction in linguistic sex differentiation appears to be taking place as an unconscious reflection of social and attitudinal changes. However, overt social movements to reduce sexual discrimination and gender-role stereotyping have also led to a number of conscious attempts to influence and change languages and linguistic behaviour. These conscious attempts have not, for the most part, focused on actual differences between the speech of men and women.

Most attention has in fact been directed at the structure and vocabulary of languages themselves. As far as English is concerned, attention has been focused, for example, on words like *chairman*. This is because words of this type appear to be discriminatory since, while they can in fact apply to people of both sexes, they are apparently male-orientated in that they contain the element *-man*. Formerly, people taking on the role of chairman were exclusively male, and the word was obviously originally a compound of *chair* and *man*. Many English speakers, however, have ceased to perceive this word as a compound and no more feel it to be composed of two units – *chair* and *man* – than they perceive *cupboard* to be composed of *cup* and *board*. (And the final syllable of *chairman* is, of course, pronounced *m'n* rather than *man*, like the final syllable of *woman*.) Nevertheless, many other speakers do perceive it as a compound, and some of them have drawn attention to its at least apparent male bias. This has led in recent years to heightened awareness of the issue, and to the increased use of clearly non-discriminatory terms such as *chair* or *chairperson* and/or, for women, *chairwoman*.

In English, as in many other languages, the traditional, formal way of pronominalizing nouns like *person* for which sex is not specified has been by the pronoun *he*, not *she*. Phrases like *the first person to finish his dinner* can refer to people of both sexes, but *the first person to finish her dinner* can refer only to females. The fact that *he* can be used in this way and *she* cannot may well reflect the traditionally male-dominated structure of our society. In recent years, speakers and writers have tried to avoid this appearance of inequality by actually using *she* in this generic way, or by employing the form *s/he* (this only works in writing, of course). Colloquial, informal English, though, has always had a very sensible way out of this problem, the use of the singular *they*: *the first person to finish their dinner*.

English also has a number of pairs of words for males and females which appear, at first sight, to be equivalent:

gentleman – lady
man – woman
boy – girl

Terms of this type have become the topic of some comment because, as closer examination will reveal, they are not equivalent at all in actual usage. Moreover, it is highly probable that the ways in which their usage differs reflect, and presumably also reinforce, different attitudes in our society to men and women and to gender roles generally. The connotations of the word *lady*, for example, are rather different from those of the word *gentleman*, and as far as usage is concerned, *lady* is in many respects actually an equivalent to *man*. Many English speakers tell their children that it is impolite to call or refer to someone as *a woman* (but not *a man*). Shop assistants in Britain may be referred to as *sales ladies* (but not *sales gentlemen*). *Ladies' wear* can be found for sale alongside *mens' wear* – and so on.

Robin Lakoff has argued that this is because *lady* is a euphemism for *woman*. A euphemism has become necessary because of the unfavourable connotations that *woman* has for some people, which is in turn because of the lower status women have typically had in our society, and because of the sexual implications the word *woman* has in a male-dominated society. (The sexual connotations become clear if you compare the two sentences: *She's only thirteen, but she's already a woman* and *She's only thirteen, but she's already a lady*.)

Similarly, *girl* and *boy* are also by no means precise equivalents. *Boy* refers of course to a young male person, but many people feel uncomfortable about using it to refer to anyone older than early teenage, and it is certainly not in very wide use for individuals aged over about twenty. On the other hand, *girl* can be used for women considerably older than this, and it is not unusual to hear of a group of people that it consisted of, say, *five men* and *six girls*. It has been, in other words, more usual to use the more childlike word for women than for men.

As we have said, the implications of this unequal usage have not escaped notice in recent years, and increased awareness of the discriminatory nature of this differentiation seems currently to be leading to a linguistic change for some speakers. A number of speakers have begun to avoid using the word *girl* to refer to adult women. For some of them, however, it is not entirely clear what they should use instead. Some young women are happy to be referred to as a *woman*, but some are not, and it is not always easy to know what reactions will be to the words *woman* and *girl*. This seems to be leading, as a way of avoiding this problem, to an increase in the usage of the word *lady* where formerly *girl* would have been more usual – and in a manner which shows that the sexual implications of *woman* have now been acquired by *lady* also, as in: *John is going out with a new lady tonight*. Lakoff writes that it would not make sense to say something like *After ten years in gaol Harry wanted to find a lady*. This would formerly indeed have been anomalous. For many younger speakers, however, it would now be quite usual.

Because language and society are so closely linked, it is possible, in some cases, to encourage social change by directing attention towards linguistic reflections of aspects of society that one would like to see altered. Then, it is hoped, language and society will both be changed. In some instances, attempts to change the language, at least, have been very successful. In the USA, for example, names for hurricanes are now equally distributed between male and female names (whereas before they were entirely female), and, perhaps more importantly, job description labels are no longer marked for sex.

In the case of *lady, woman* and *girl*, however, the linguistic change achieved seems, for some speakers at least, not to have been the one desired. Traditionally, *man* has been used more often than *woman*, while *lady* and *girl* have been employed more often than *gentleman* and *boy*. Conscious attempts at change have been directed at reducing the use of *girl* (as demeaning for adult women) and of *lady* (as a trivializing euphemism), and at increasing the usage of the less discriminatory *woman*. It is quite possible, however, that in future it will actually be the term *lady* that will see an increase in usage. Linguistic changes follow social changes very readily, but it is not always a simple matter to make them *precede* social changes.

Sociolinguistic research has also revealed that there are tendencies towards interesting differences in the conversational styles used by men and women. We are leaving a discussion of this, however, to Chapter 6.

5. Language and Context

Language, like other forms of social activity, has to be appropriate to the speaker using it. This is why, in many communities, men's and women's speech is different. This, however, is only a part of the overall picture. Behaviour does not only have to be appropriate to the individual, it also needs to be suitable for particular occasions and situations. This, too, has its counterpart in language. To give a boxing commentary in the language of the Bible or a parish-church sermon in legal language would be either a bad mistake, or a joke. Language, in other words, varies not only according to the social characteristics of speakers (such as social class, ethnic group, age and sex) but also according to the social context in which they find themselves. The same speaker uses different linguistic varieties in different situations and for different purposes. The totality of linguistic varieties used in this way – and they may be very many – by a particular community of speakers can be called that linguistic community's *verbal repertoire*.

Many social factors can come into play in controlling which variety from this verbal repertoire is actually to be used on a particular occasion. For example, if speakers are talking to the people they work with about their work, their language is likely to be rather different from that they will use, say, at home with their families. Linguistic varieties that are linked in this way to occupations, professions or topics have been termed *registers*. The register of law, for example, is different from the register of medicine, which in turn is different from the language of engineering – and so on. Registers are usually characterized solely by vocabulary differences: either by the use of particular words, or by the use of words in a particular sense. For example, bus-company employees, at least in certain parts of Britain, are much more likely to call buses with two decks *deckers*, while lay people will generally refer to them as *double-deckers*. Similarly, professional soccer players and lay people both discuss football. The footballers, however, are much more likely, in Britain, to refer to the playing area as *the park* than lay people, who are probably more likely to call it *the pitch*. Many other examples of the same sort of phenomena could be cited.

Registers are simply a rather special case of a particular kind of language being produced by the social situation. Many other factors connected with the situation in which language is being used, over and above occupation, will also have a linguistic effect. Language varies, for example, according to whether it is written or spoken. Other things being equal, written English tends to be more formal than spoken English, and the same sort of differences occur in other languages. In French the simple preterite (past historic) tense, as in *il donna* 'he gave', is used in even the most popular detective fiction, but is rarer in speech, where the perfect form *il a donné* is normally used instead. In some languages the differences may be much greater. In Tamil and in other Indian languages there is a clear and rather considerable difference between a literary variety of the language and a colloquial variety. (This means that, as in the case of some other languages we shall be discussing below, writing is an art which takes many years of formal education to acquire.)

Similarly, the kind of subject matter that is under discussion will have an effect, in addition to that of register, on the language produced. Topics such as molecular biology or international economics are likely to produce linguistic varieties which are more formal than those used in the discussion of knitting or roller-skating. The physical setting and occasion of the language activity will also have some consequences. For instance, academic lectures and ceremonial occasions are more likely to select relatively formal language than, say, public-house arguments or family breakfasts. Linguistic varieties that are linked in this way to the formality of the situation can be termed *styles*, and can be thought of as being sited along a scale ranging from formal to informal. Styles and registers are in principle independent. The register of football, for example, could co-occur with a formal style (as in a report in a high-status newspaper), or with an informal style (as in a discussion in a bar). Often, however, as in the case of international economics or roller-skating, they will be linked.

A further important feature of the social context is the 'context' of the person spoken to, and in particular the role relationships and relative statuses of the participants in a discourse. For example, speech between individuals of un-equal rank (due to status in an organization, social class, age, or some other factor) is likely to be less relaxed and more formal than that between equals, and in certain languages definite rules may exist as to which linguistic forms may or may not be used. A good example of this is the different forms of *address* that are produced by different degrees of status difference or intimacy. Different degrees of politeness and deference may be required, and these are signalled linguistically. The connotations of English address-forms such as *sir, Mr Smith, Smith, Frederick, Fred, mate* and so on, are all different. Each has different stylistic implications, and the rules for their usage, as well as the frequency of their usage, are quite complex. These rules often vary from class to class, age-group to age-group, and place to place. There are notable differences between the usage of British and American speakers of English, for example: the term *sir*, for instance, is used more freely as a term of address – to attract someone's attention, for instance – in the United States than in Britain. In some cases there may be considerable uncertainty as to which form is the appropriate one to use – many British people are not certain as to what they should call their parents-in-law, for example – and this may well result in no address-form being used at all.

In languages other than English the position may also be complicated by the problem of personal pronoun selection. Most European (and many other) languages, for instance, unlike English which has only *you*, distinguish, especially in the singular, between a polite and a familiar second-person pronoun:

	familiar	polite
French	*tu*	*vous*
Italian	*tu*	*Lei*
Spanish	*tú*	*usted*
German	*du*	*Sie*
Dutch	*jij*	*u*
Swedish	*du*	*ni*
Norwegian	*du*	*De*
Greek	*esi*	*esis*
Russian	*ty*	*vy*

It has been argued that, originally, the familiar pronouns were the normal form of address for single individuals, and the polite forms either second-person plural or third-person pronouns (Stage 1 – see p. 89). However, the habit grew up amongst the upper classes in medieval times of showing respect for a person by addressing them with what are now the polite pronouns (following the French forms, we can refer to the familiar pronouns collectively as T, the polite forms as V). This aristocratic habit led to a situation where, although the upper classes called each other V and the lower classes used T amongst themselves, the upper classes used T to the lower classes who, on the other hand, called them V (Stage 2). This can be interpreted as signifying that where a difference of *power* was involved (the aristocracy having power in the community) in a meeting between two individuals, then pronoun usage was *non-reciprocal*: those with power used T to those without, but received V back, much as a schoolteacher today in most parts of the English-speaking world may call a child *Johnny* but be called *Mr Smith* in return.

Subsequently, however, another feature of the social relationship began to have some influence on pronoun selection. Following Roger Brown and Albert Gilman, who have carried out valuable research into T- and V-usage which we shall discuss below, we can call this factor *solidarity*. It seems that the usage of V, which when employed by the power-less to the power-ful signified a difference of power, became generalized to symbolize *all* types of social difference and distance. As a result of this new factor, T-usage now became more probable when the degree of intimacy, similarity or solidarity between speakers was felt to be quite large. This meant that, while the non-reciprocal T–V-usage remained in discourse between unequals, equals now addressed each other as *either* T *or* V, depending on the degree of intimacy or solidarity involved (Stage 3). In two cases this led to a conflict. Where someone of high rank addressed someone of low rank with whom they were not intimate, such as, for instance, a customer addressing a waiter, then the power factor would suggest T, but the new solidarity factor V. And where a person of inferior rank addressed a superior with whom they *were* intimate, such as a child addressing a parent, then the power factor would indicate V, but the solidarity factor T. In both these cases, in most European languages, the solidarity factor has now won out over the power factor, so that pronoun usage is nearly always reciprocal. For example, instead of an officer calling a soldier T but receiving V, both now use V, because the relationship, in both directions, is not one of solidarity. And instead of an older brother calling a younger brother T but receiving V, both now use T (Stage 4).

Solidarity, presumably because of the gradual rise of democratic egalitarian ideology, has today become the major factor involved. There are still, however, some interesting differences between language communities in T- and V-usage. Brown and Gilman have investigated the extent of T- and V-usage by students from different European and other countries. They found that relationships such as father–son, customer–waiter, boss–clerk were never 'power coded' in modern French, German or Italian. Pronoun usage is now always reciprocal, although formerly this would not have been the case. Afrikaans speakers, on the other hand, *did* make several non-reciprocal power-coded distinctions in these situations. This,

	Stage 1		Stage 2		Stage 3		Stage 4	
	S	NS	S	NS	S	NS	S	NS
a) $+P \rightarrow +P$	T	T	V	V	T	V	T	V
b) $-P \rightarrow -P$	T	T	T	T	T	V	T	V
c) $+P \rightarrow -P$	T	T	T	T	T	*T*	T	V
d) $-P \rightarrow +P$	T	T	V	V	*V*	V	T	V

P = power   S = solidarity   NS = no solidarity

Stage 1: original situation, only singular and plural distinguished.

Stage 2: introduction of the power factor, non-reciprocal usage between c) and d).

Stage 3: introduction of the solidarity factor, points of conflict of the two factors italicized.

Stage 4: resolution today of the conflict in favour of the solidarity factor.

according to Brown and Gilman, signifies a 'less developed egalitarian ethic' on the part of Afrikaans speakers. From their work and from other sources, it also appears that French and Italian speakers are more likely to use T to acquaintances than German speakers; that German speakers are more likely to use T to distant relations; Norwegian schoolchildren are more likely than Dutch or German pupils to use T to their teachers (indeed some Norwegian pupils also address their teachers by their first names); male Italians are more likely to use T to female fellow students; and that, generally, Italians use more T than the French, who in turn use more T than the Germans. Similar differences were noted by Brown and Gilman between individuals: other things being equal, politically more conservative speakers tended to use fewer T forms than others.

In other linguistic communities further complications arise, since it is not only names or address pronouns that are involved. In both Japanese and Korean, for example, the context of the person addressed can, in addition to particular address-forms, produce rather considerable grammatical and lexical variation as well, depending on the relationship between and the relative statuses of the two people involved. A Korean speaker, for instance, may have to choose one out of six different verb suffixes, depending on their relationship to the person addressed. Unlike English address-forms, moreover, the issue cannot be evaded by 'no-naming' or not selecting an alternative, since verbs may, grammatically, *require* suffixes. In fact, verb forms in Korean may have one of the following suffixes attached to them:

> intimate: *-na*
> familiar: *-e*
> plain: *-ta*
> polite: *-e yo*
> deferential: *-supnita*
> authoritative: *-so*

In other languages restrictions on linguistic forms according to the context of the person addressed may go even further than this. In Javanese, for example, there are several distinct speech 'levels', or varieties which are used in different situations, which involve not only minor differences of pronouns and suffixes but also numerous lexical differences. The levels are relatively discrete, and have names that are well-known in the community. Co-occurrence restrictions also occur at each level: given that a word which belongs to a particular speech level occurs, then only other words from the same level may follow. As with European T and V pronouns, the use of a particular level depends both on the familiarity of the speakers and on their relative statuses. Very often, moreover, the usage is not reciprocal. As an example of the nature of the differences involved, we can cite three different levels of the 'same' sentence as described by Clifford Geertz. These levels all occur in the slightly educated form of a town dialect of Javanese:

'Are you going to eat rice and cassava now?'
1. *Menapa pandjenengan baḍé ḍahar sekul kalijan kaspé samenika.*
2. *Napa sampéjan adjeng neda sekul lan kaspé saniki.*
3. *Apa kowé arep mangan sega lan kaspé saiki.*

Sentence 1 is the high (formal) level and 3 the low (informal) level. Only the word *kaspé* is common to all three levels, although two others occur at two levels and some words appear to be related to each other.

Many aspects of the social situation, then, can contribute to deciding which linguistic variety is to be employed on a particular occasion, while the styles and registers which make up speakers' verbal repertoires are the particular versions of their dialects which they use in particular contexts for particular topics. As we have seen, styles range from the formal to the informal. Pronouns of the V type signal a relatively formal style, as do the Javanese high level and the Korean polite suffixes. 'Formality' is not, in fact, something which it is easy to define with any degree of precision, largely because it subsumes very many factors including familiarity, kinship-relationship, politeness, seriousness, and so on, but most people have a good idea of the relative formality and informality of particular linguistic variants in their own language. It is not difficult, for example, to decide upon the relative formality of the following pairs of sentences:

> *I require your attendance to be punctual.*
> *I want you to come on time.*
>
> *Father was somewhat fatigued after his lengthy journey.*
> *Dad was pretty tired after his long trip.*
>
> *A not inconsiderable amount of time was expended on the task.*
> *The job took a long time.*

Styles of this type in English are characterized by vocabulary differences (*tired* as opposed to *fatigued*; *trip* as opposed to *journey*) but also, as the last pair of sentences show, by syntactic differences – the passive voice is much more frequent in formal styles in English. These styles resemble the levels of Javanese, which are also signalled by vocabulary differences, but the parallel is not complete, since the same sort of strict co-occurrence restrictions do not operate in English. It is quite possible, for instance, to say:

> *Dad was pretty fatigued after his long trip.*

Another important aspect of situational variation in English is that, as in other languages, not only grammar and vocabulary are involved. As many English speakers shift, according to situation, along the scale of formality, their *pronunciation* changes as well. The actual nature of these 'phonological styles' is rather interesting. The urban dialect surveys of English that we have already discussed (p. 31ff.) were concerned, amongst other things, to relate linguistic variables to the social characteristics of the speaker. They were also, however, interested in the relationship between these variables and social context. It was known, of course, that speakers change their pronunciation from situation to situation (most people know someone who has a 'telephone voice', for example) but there were problems as to how to investigate what form this change took. One obvious difficulty was that, since the data obtained in these surveys was elicited by means of an interview, the style of pronunciation used by informants was largely that variety appropriate to *a tape-recorded interview with a stranger*. The style of speech recorded was, therefore, rather formal compared to everyday conversation.

In his New York study, however, Labov overcame this problem and his methodology has subsequently been followed by others. By using, as a controlling factor, the amount of attention paid to speech at any time during the interview, he found that it was possible to produce the equivalent of distinct contextual styles of pronunciation. The main body of conversation obtained in the interviews, because of the artificiality and formality of the situation, contained speech that had more attention directed towards it by the speaker than is normal in everyday speech with close acquaintances. Informants knew their speech was being studied, and were therefore 'on their guard' as far as their pronunciation was concerned. This style of pronunciation has therefore been termed *formal speech*. In certain parts of the interview, however, attempts were made to elicit other styles. At one point, for example, the formality of style was increased by asking the informants to read aloud from a specially prepared reading passage. This produced a style that was even more formal, because reading aloud is a special case, as it were, of written rather than spoken language and, secondly, because reading is a specialized linguistic activity where speakers pay considerable attention to the way they are speaking. Then the informant also read aloud from a list of individual words. Here the pronunciation was a degree more formal again, since the attention of the reader was concentrated on a single word at a time, a much simpler reading task. In this way, then, three different formal styles of pronunciation were obtained.

What, however, of 'normal', informal speech? Attempts were made to elicit, in spite of the artificial interview situation, normal casual speech such as the informant would use in everyday conversation with friends and family. Several ways emerged in which this could be done. Casual speech might occur, in the first place, outside the context of the interview, as in conversation with other members of the family who might be present, or in breaks for a coffee or beer. And it was also found that certain questions asked during the interview itself were likely to produce casual speech as a response. Labov, for example, asked his informants if they had ever been in a situation where they thought they were in danger of being killed. Generally informants who related such an incident became emotionally involved in the narrative and, in attempting to convince the interviewer of the reality of the danger, forgot the formal constraints of the interview situation.

In this way four different styles of pronunciation were obtained ranging from the informal, casual speech, through formal speech and reading-passage style, to the most formal, word-list style. This means that scores obtained by informants for particular linguistic variables can be related to interview style and so, by implication, to social context, as well as to social class. We saw earlier how usage of the *-ing* variable in Norwich English was clearly related to social class. We can now supplement this information with data on stylistic variation as well. Table 10 shows the percentage of non-RP *-in'* endings used in words like *walking* and *hoping* by the five social classes in the four contextual styles: word-list style

Table 10. -in' forms used in four contextual styles in Norwich

	WLS	RPS	FS	CS
MMC	0%	0%	3%	28%
LMC	0	10	15	42
UWC	5	15	74	87
MWC	23	44	88	95
LWC	29	66	98	100

(WLS); reading-passage style (RPS); formal speech (FS); and casual speech (CS). The twenty scores shown there form a perfect pattern. Scores rise consistently from WLS to CS, and from MMC to LWC, and range from 0 per cent, signifying consistent use of *-ing*, to 100 per cent, signifying, on the part of the LWC in CS, consistent use of *-in'*. This indicates that, just as in more formal contexts speakers are more likely to use words such as *fatigued* and grammatical features such as the passive voice, so speakers of all classes increase the percentage of high-status RP *-ing* forms in their speech in the same contexts. It is interesting to note that, although the different social class groups have different levels of *-ing* usage, their evaluation of the two variants is exactly the same. All classes change their pronunciation in exactly the same direction so that, for example, the MMC in their everyday conversation use, on average, the same amount of non-RP forms as the LWC do in their most formal style.

In some cases this shifting – with lower classes using, in formal styles, speech characteristics of higher classes in informal speech – can have interesting effects. We have already noted the different percentages of non-prevocalic /r/ used by speakers from different social-class backgrounds in New York. Figure 4 shows that the overall pattern of class and style differentiation for /r/ follows the same outline as the Norwich *-ing* scores, *except at one point*. The figure shows a steady rise in the use of prestige forms as formality of style increases, so that in formal styles lower-class speech approaches higher-class informal speech. The one exception is, as shown in the cross-over pattern, that the LMC in WLS

% /r/ pronounced

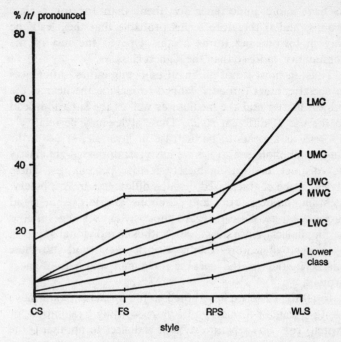

Figure 4. Social-class and style differentiation of non-prevocalic /r/ in New York City (after Labov)

uses more /r / than the highest class. In this style the normal pattern of class differentiation is upset. In trying to achieve the prestige style of pronunciation used by the highest class, we can say, the LMC, in the style where most attention is paid to speech, go beyond this level – they overdo it. This kind of linguistic behaviour on the part of the LMC suggests that they are, as the *second* highest class, linguistically and presumably socially somewhat insecure. Because of this linguistic insecurity they pay more attention to speech than other classes, and the degree of style-shifting amongst this group is therefore greater than amongst other classes. This suggests, further, that this particular social group may be instrumental in introducing prestige features such as non-prevocalic /r / into particular dialects. Prestige features appear to have more importance for them than for other class groups, and it therefore seems probable that they lead the way in introducing forms of this type to the rest of the community, more so than the highest class.

Thus, in most if not all linguistic communities, differences in social context (broadly defined to include the hearer, the subject matter and the medium as well as the situation) lead to the use of different styles. These styles may be relatively discrete, as appears to be the case in Javanese, or not – the English phonological styles we have just discussed are clearly not distinct, comprising merely relative percentages. These styles can be characterized through differences in vocabulary, including address-forms and pronouns, and in grammar and pronunciation. We can regard these styles as being varieties within dialects, since they occur, within an individual's speech, as a result of features of the social context, and still show characteristics of the speaker's regional and social background.

In all the cases we have noted so far, speakers either move along a scale of formality of style, according to situation, or switch from one separate style of a dialect to another – the situational varieties or styles are clearly sub-varieties of one regional and/or social dialect. Elsewhere, however, situational switching must take place *between* different dialects. (Here we must bear in mind the concepts of discreteness and continuity we discussed in Chapter 1 – the difference between the two types of switching is more one of degree than of kind.) In these cases, one dialect will occur in formal situations, and another in informal situations. For example, native speakers of Lowland Scots dialects may switch, in relatively formal situations, to Standard English (spoken with a Scots accent, of course). It is legitimate to regard this situation as rather different from that of an English speaker from England who simply switches styles. In the first place, the difference between the linguistic varieties involved in the switching is much greater. Secondly, as in the case of levels in Javanese, co-occurrence restrictions are involved: it is not usual to use Lowland Scots forms when speaking Standard English, or vice versa. And thirdly, whereas other English speakers switch from one variety of their vernacular to another, Scots dialect speakers switch from their own vernacular to that of others – a linguistic variety that they normally learn only at school. There is thus probably no question, in the case of many Scots speakers, of being able to shift along a scale of formality. Rather, they will have to switch over in formal situations to a similar but nevertheless completely distinct variety. The jump from, for example, Scots dialect:

> [av kɛnt jon man eçt jirz]
> *I've kenned yon man eight years.*

to standard Scots English:

> [av non ðat man et jirz]
> *I've known that man eight years.*

is quite considerable, and requires, on the part of children in school, (a) the learning of new words, in this case *know*; (b) the learning of new pronunciations, such as [et]; and (c) the replacement of one known word by another: *yon* becomes *that*. The differences between the style-switching of a Londoner and that of a Scots dialect speaker, simply as far as pronunciation is concerned, are notable:

	informal	formal	informal	formal
one	[jɪn]	[wʌn]	[wʌn]	[wʌn]
two	[twɔ]	[tʉ]	[tʉː]	[tʉː]
three	[θri]	[θri]	[fɹiː]	[θɹiː]
eight	[eçt]	[et]	[æɪt]	[ɛɪt]
	A SCOTS DIALECT		A LONDON ACCENT	

In other parts of the world, dialect-switching of the Lowland-Scots–Standard-English type may take on a rather different form. In some communities, for example, switching is carried out on a much larger and more institutionalized scale. This sociolinguistic situation has been called *diglossia*. *Diglossia* is a particular kind of language standardization where two distinct varieties of a language exist side by side *throughout* the speech community (not just in the case of a particular group of speakers, such as working-class Scots), and where each of the two varieties is assigned a definite social function. (Since the term *diglossia* was first introduced by Charles Ferguson, it has been extended by some writers to include any situation where switching between two varieties takes place, but I prefer to retain the insights concerning the rather special nature of the situations indicated by the original use, and use the term as just defined.) The two linguistic varieties in a diglossic situation are considered by speakers to be discrete, although this is usually not altogether the case in practice, and comprise a standardized *high* variety and a *low* variety which can also be standardized but may be subject to geographical differentiation too. The two varieties have overt recognition in the community, and have commonly known and used labels. Examples of language communities which are diglossic, together with the names used, are the following:

	High	*Low*
Swiss German:	Hochdeutsch	Schweizerdeutsch
Arabic:	classical	colloquial
Tamil:	literary	colloquial

The most important feature of the diglossic situation is probably the specialization of function of the two varieties. This varies from community to community, but typically the high variety is used in sermons, formal letters, political speeches, university lectures, news broadcasts, newspaper editorials, and 'high' poetry. The low variety, on the other hand, is used in conversation with family and friends, radio serials, political and academic discussions, political cartoons, and 'folk' literature. At other points the linguistic communities vary.

The main differences between diglossic and other situations, then, are that the low diglossic variety is standardized, to varying extents (Schweizerdeutsch and regional colloquial Arabic are both used on the radio, for instance); that the two varieties have names and are felt to be distinct; that the situations where each is to be used are socially fairly well defined; and – and this is of great importance – no section of the community regularly uses the high variety as the normal medium of everyday conversation (this distinguishes it from the English situation, for instance). The high variety has in all cases to be learnt as a school language. This is why the situations where the high variety is used involve either written language or, if spoken language is involved, tend to be situations where preparation is possible. Where, in isolated cases, individuals do attempt to use the high variety in everyday speech this is generally felt to be artificial, pedantic, snobbish or reactionary. In German Switzerland it may also be felt to be disloyal, since the high variety, Standard German, *is* used as the medium of everyday conversation by speakers *outside* Switzerland. Generally speaking, the high variety has greater prestige than the low, and is often regarded as more beautiful, even if it is less intelligible. In Arabic, for instance, it has been considered good form by some to write an editorial or poem containing rare or old-fashioned expressions which no one can understand without consulting a dictionary.

Linguistically speaking, the differences between the high and low varieties in the diglossic situation may be considerable. Many of the differences are vocabulary differences: many pairs of words may occur, referring to common objects or concepts, where the meaning is roughly the same, but where the usage of one item rather than another immediately indicates high or low variety. For example, in Arabic the form [ra²aː] *to see* indicates the high classical variety, [šaːf] the low variety. There are generally grammatical differences, too. The phonology will also often vary. In Arabic the two phonologies are quite different, and in Swiss German very different.

As far as Arabic in general is concerned, the sociolinguistic relationship of the two varieties varies today from country to country. The classical variety is still generally the predominant written language, although colloquial Arabic can now also be written, especially in novels and letters, and there is a tendency for different standards based on regional low varieties to arise in each country. On the other hand, although it is still possible to *speak* the high variety (particularly in lectures, for example) this is increasingly less usual. In normal educated speech there is often a mixture: mainly colloquial Arabic, but with an admixture of classical elements. To give some idea of the nature of the linguistic differences involved, we can cite the following examples of some of the contrasts that occurred in a short paragraph of a book written in classical Arabic, together with the colloquial Egyptian equivalents.

	High	*Low*
'I say'	[aquːl]	[aʔʌːl]
'I cannot'	[laʔastətiʕ]	[maʔdarš]
'many'	[kaθirah]	[kətir]
'that'	[ðaːkə]	[da]

The diglossic differences between the two types of Arabic can thus be seen to involve the use of different words, together with the substitution of some sounds for others. The following correspondences, for instance, appear to occur in the above examples:

[q] corresponds to [ʔ]
[θ] corresponds to [t]
[ð] corresponds to [d]

The situation in German Switzerland differs somewhat from the Arabic situation. Schweizerdeutsch is widely used on Swiss radio, but there is no real agreed standardization. In spite of a tendency to iron out regional differences, as in town speech, many different regional dialects are still widely used by speakers from all social backgrounds. The high variety, Standard German, is used, as a spoken language, in parliament, in courts, churches, universities and the higher forms of schools, and in interaction with Germans, Austrians, and non-native German speakers. It is, however, spoken with Swiss phonology and phonetics, and contains a number of regionalisms (rather in the fashion of standard Scots English), and is therefore markedly different from the spoken Standard German of Germany. Otherwise the high variety serves as the *written* language. (There *is* a notable body of literature in Schweizerdeutsch, but much of it is of the somewhat self-conscious dialect-literature type.) Swiss German dialects, on the other hand, are the normal medium of everyday conversation for Swiss Germans of all social backgrounds. As an illustration of the nature of the differences involved, we cite the following passage in the low variety, in this case a dialect text based on Zurich speech, with an accompanying equivalent in the high Standard German variety. Even from the orthography it can be seen that the phonology is very different, and there are several differences of grammatical construction. There are also some vocabulary differences. *Möödeli*, for example, corresponds to Standard German *Gewohnheiten*. Mostly, however, the lexical items in the two passages are related to each other: we can say, for instance, that *tüütsch* and *deutsch* are the 'same word'.

Low variety – Swiss German:

En Schwyzer isch er zwaar nie woorde, weder en papiirige na äine im Hëërz ine; und eebigs häd mer syner Spraach aagmërkt, das er nüd daa uufgwachsen ischt. Nüd nu s Muul häd de Usslländer verraate, au syni Möödteli. Er häd lieber mit syne tüütsche Landslüüte weder mit de Yhäimische vercheert, und ischt Mitgliid und Zaalmäischter von irem Veräin gsy.

High Variety – Standard German:

Ein Schweizer ist er zwar nie geworden, weder auf dem Papier noch im Herzen; und man hat es seine Sprache angemerkt, dass er nicht dort aufgewachsen ist. Nicht nur die Sprache hat den Ausländer verraten, sondern auch seine Gewohnheiten. Er hat lieber mit seinen deutschen Landsleuten als mit den Einheimischen verkehrt, und ist Mitglied und Zahlmeister ihres Vereins gewesen.

English:

'He never actually became Swiss, neither on paper nor in his heart; and you could tell from his language that he had not grown up there. It was not only his language that showed that he was a foreigner – his way of life showed it too. He preferred to associate with his German compatriots rather than with the natives, and was a member and the treasurer of their society.'

This gives some indication of the educational problems

faced by Swiss German children, who must learn Standard German in addition to acquiring literacy. The acquisition of Standard German, however, makes Swiss German children members of the wider German-speaking community, and gives them access to a language of wider communication and to German literature and publications.

A similar situation to that of German Switzerland obtains in Luxemburg. Here too the vernacular of the majority of the inhabitants is a dialect of German. As a focus of national loyalties this dialect has, as a low variety in a diglossic situation, a status far above that of German dialects in Germany. Many Luxemburgers, in fact, consider it to be completely distinct from German, and there have been official moves in recent years to afford it full status as a language. The position in Luxemburg is, however, complicated by the fact that, in addition to the Standard German which acts as a high variety, French also plays an important role in Luxemburg society. Luxemburgish is not often written (although there are some children's books, dialect literature and newspaper articles) and there is no real agreement as to a writing system. Children who have Luxemburgish as their vernacular have to learn to read and write in German when they go to school. Gradually German is also introduced as the *medium* of instruction until, in the last years of school, and often also in higher education, it is replaced by French. This obviously places children in Luxemburg under considerable linguistic strain. On the other hand it also means that most educated Luxemburgers are trilingual (at least) and it gives them access to two 'world languages' through which they can gain contact with academic and other literature, and communicate with foreigners when they travel outside their country. French is the official parliamentary language in Luxemburg, as well as the language of higher education. Public signs and notices tend to be in French; books, newspapers and letters in German; and everyday speech in Luxemburgish. (It is also notable that the Luxemburgish spoken by students tends often to have some admixture of French, rather than of German words.) The following short passage, taken from a newspaper article, illustrates some of the differences between Luxemburgish and Standard German as it is used in Luxemburg. These differences, which are lexical, grammatical and phonological, demonstrate the nature of the difficulties faced by Luxemburg children in school:

Luxemburgish:
> *Wéi de Rodange 1872 säi Buch drécke gelooss huet, du bluf hien drop sëtzen. En hat e puer Leit ze luusség op d'Zéiwe getrëppelt, déi dat net verquësst hun. Eréischt eng Generation doerno huet de Rodange ugefaang séng giedléch Plaz ze kréien. Séng Kanner hu wéinstens nach erlieft, wéi 1927 eng Grimmel vun deem gutt gemaach guf, wat un him verbrach gi wor!*

Standard German:
> *Als Rodange 1872 sein Buch drucken liess, hatte er keinen Erfolg damit. Mit zuviel List war er ein paar Leuten auf die Zehen getreten, und die konnten ihm das nicht verzeihen. Erst eine Generation später begann Rodange, seinen ihm zustehenden Platz zu erhalten. Seine Kinder haben es wenigstens noch erlebt, dass 1927 ein wenig von dem gut gemacht wurde, was an ihm verbrochen worden war!*

English:
> 'When Rodange had his book printed in 1872 he had no success with it. With too much intrigue he had trodden on some people's toes, and they could not forgive him that. Only a generation later did Rodange begin to receive his rightful place. His children at least experienced the making good, in 1927, of some of the wrong that had been done him.'

How stable are diglossic situations? Interesting light is shed on this question by what has happened recently in the case of Greek. Until at least the 1970s, Greek was a diglossic language, with a high variety, Katharevousa, which harked back to the glories of the classical and Byzantine past, and Dhimotiki, which resembled the modern spoken language much more closely. The two varieties differed considerably in vocabulary and morphology. During this century, there was very considerable tension about which of the two varieties should be the language of government and education with, to simplify considerably, Katharevousa attracting more support from the political right, Dhimotiki from the left. The right-wing military junta which seized power in a coup in 1967 was particularly heavy-handed in imposing Katharevousa. This has had the effect, since the restoration of democracy in Greece, of totally discrediting Katharevousa, which has now almost completely disappeared: Greek is no longer really diglossic. Interestingly, however, the form of Dhimotiki now in most widespread use does show quite a lot of linguistic influence from Katharevousa.

We have seen, then, that a community's verbal repertoire may encompass simply different styles of the same dialect, as in the case of Standard-English speakers; different dialects of the same language, as in the case of Lowland Scots speakers; or, as a special case of the latter, two relatively standardized varieties in a diglossic relationship, as in the case of Arabic. (It is also possible that where, in the diglossic case, the low variety is considerably standardized, the two phenomena may be combined: a speaker may switch from local dialect to low standard to high standard, according to the situation – many Arabic speakers command three varieties in this way.)

In the case of Luxemburg, however, we saw a further complication introduced. Here the diglossic situation is combined with another sociolinguistic activity we can call *language-switching*. So far we have been discussing the way in which speakers switch from one variety to another which is linguistically more or less closely related: formal English, informal English; Scots dialect, Standard English; colloquial Arabic, classical Arabic. In many communities, however, the verbal repertoire may contain varieties which are not related; different languages, we can say. As in Luxemburg, where switching occurs between German and French, *language-*switching will take place, like style- or dialect-switching, according to the social situation. (In fact, in some places, all three different types of switching may be involved. The verbal repertoire of many educated speakers in Delhi, for instance, comprises English, a clearly distinct language, as well as Urdu and Hindi, which are considered separate languages but which are very similar, *and* some relatively very different styles of Hindi.)

Paraguay is one of the places where research has been carried out into the nature of language-switching of this sort. Here the two languages involved are Spanish and Guarani, an indigenous American Indian language. Guarani has been reported as being the vernacular of 88 per cent of the population, approximately, and Spanish of only 6 per cent, but a high percentage know and use both, and both are official languages. Paraguay is unusual in Latin America, since this type of bilingualism has usually indicated a transitional stage leading to Spanish monolingualism. In Paraguay, however, 92 per cent of the population know Guarani, and most speakers continue to use it after learning Spanish. Bilingualism, that is, appears to be a permanent feature of the society. Many features of the social situation seem to be involved in determining which language is to be used. Perhaps the main determinant is the geographical location of a conversation. If this takes place in a rural area, then Guarani is employed. Spanish is not really necessary in the countryside, although it is used in speaking to the village schoolteacher, and is taught and used in school. (Guarani, on the other hand, is not strictly necessary in towns. It is, however, undoubtedly an asset, and anyone unable to speak it would be socially isolated to a certain extent.) In urban areas, though, the position is more complicated. If, for instance, the occasion, or the relationship between the participants, is a *formal* one, then the language used is Spanish. If, however, it is *informal*, then other factors come into play, notably the degree of *intimacy*. If the relationship between speakers is not an intimate one, then Spanish is used (it is said that courting couples begin in Spanish, for example!). But if the relationship *is* an intimate one, then the language used will depend, as in other cases we have already examined, on the topic of conversation. Jokes are always in Guarani, whereas if the topic is a serious one, then the language used will generally be the *mother tongue* (first language learnt) of the speaker concerned (although he or she will make allowances for the language proficiency of the hearer). Sex may also come into play as a factor here. *Men* for whom Spanish is the first language may still often use Guarani in such situations when speaking to other men. Thus, where in English factors of this sort would produce different styles, in Paraguay they produce different languages.

6. Language and Social Interaction

In the previous chapter we examined the relationship between language and social context. It is important to note, however, that language-switching and shifting are not solely *determined* by the social situation. As social psychologists of language have pointed out, speakers are not *sociolinguistic automata*. They can use switching for their own purposes: to influence or define the situation as they wish, and to convey nuances of meaning and personal intention. This can be done in one of two ways. It may, for instance, be done by, as it were, using two languages at once. For example, in many areas of the south-western USA there are many Mexican-American communities that are bilingual. Their verbal repertoires comprise Spanish and English. The following passage, demonstrating this kind of instant switching, was recorded by John Gumperz and Eduardo Hernandez from a speaker who lives in such a community, and is taken from a discussion on giving up smoking:

> I didn't quit, I just stopped. I mean it wasn't an effort I made *que voy a dejar de fumar porque me hace daño o* this or that. I used to pull butts out of the wastepaper basket. I'd get desperate, *y ahi voy al basurero a buscar, a sacar*, you know?

(The two Spanish passages can be translated as: 'that I'm going to stop smoking because it's harmful to me' and 'and there I go to the waste-basket to look for some, to get some'.) This switching, in a culture where English is the dominant language, is presumably subconscious, and has the effect of making the conversation, amongst other things, more intimate and confidential. *Language mixing*, as we can call this rapid switching, also has the effect, as the British sociolinguist Le

Page has pointed out, of enabling a speaker to signal two identities at once. For example, Chinese students at the University of Hong Kong often speak a dense mixture of English and Cantonese. If they spoke only English, they might be regarded as being disloyal to their community. If they spoke only Cantonese, they might be regarded, within the context of an English-language university, as uneducated and unsophisticated. Speaking both languages together overcomes both these problems.

The second possibility is that a speaker can switch completely from one language to another. David Parkin has described an interesting example of this from Uganda. Uganda is a multilingual country where language-switching takes place according to the social situation, as in Paraguay, but where, as in the Mexican-American example, it can also be used to communicate intentions and nuances over and above the actual verbal message. In Kampala, the capital of Uganda, the sociolinguistic situation is very complex. There are many different ethnic groups living in the town, most of them speaking different languages. Some of the groups are indigenous to Uganda, and others come from Kenya, Sudan and Zaire. In two housing estates which Parkin studied, many different vernaculars are spoken. They include six main groups of *Nilotic* languages; eleven main *Bantu* languages, six of them local and five from eastern Uganda and Kenya; *Arabic*, spoken by Moslems originally from the Sudan; two main groups of *Sudanic* languages; and a small number of speakers of *Nilo-Hamitic* languages. One of the local Bantu languages is *Luganda*. This is the language of the Ganda, who are the ethnic group indigenous to Kampala and are socially dominant in the area. Although most Ganda actually prefer not to live on the housing estates, Luganda is widely understood and spoken by non-Ganda on these estates. Two other languages also play an important role, in spite of the fact that they are not indigenous vernaculars. The people who live on the estates are relatively highly educated, and therefore know and use English, and Swahili is also widely known and used. (Originally Swahili was introduced, for the most part, by

Kenyans and Sudan Moslems, but it is now used by many Ugandans, except the Ganda, who tend to see it as undermining their position of dominance.)

This means that many people in Kampala, on these two housing estates and doubtless elsewhere, are often presented with interesting problems of language choice. The position is clearly more complicated than in Paraguay, since many people can speak English, Swahili and Luganda as well as their own vernacular, but the social situation is naturally, once again, a determining factor. Tenants-association meetings, for example, are conducted in English and Luganda in the more prestigious of the two housing estates, and in English and Swahili on the other estate. Language-choice, on the other hand, can also be employed to indicate particular moods and intentions, as we have already seen, and in Kampala the choice is wider than in the Mexican-American communities. A male, an immigrant from Kenya who was a native speaker of a Bantu language was observed one evening to meet another Kenyan. The second Kenyan was a speaker of an unrelated Nilotic language. They could not, therefore, converse in their vernaculars, but there still remained a choice of which language they should actually use. In fact the selection of a language seems to have depended, as in other cases we have discussed above, on the topic of discussion. The discussion centred round the fact that the first Kenyan had lost his job, and on, in general, the difficulties facing Kenyans in Uganda. The speakers were, in other words, discussing problems which affected them both. The language they actually used was Swahili. This appears to have been the appropriate language for commiseration, since it was symbolic of their status as equals and of their fraternal relationship. If, on the other hand, the topic had been one involving competition for prestige, such as boasting about money or girls, then they would probably have used English, which would have worked just as well from a purely verbal communication point of view.

Later on the same evening the first Kenyan met a neighbour of his who, although ethnically a Bantu like himself, was a

Ugandan, and who held, moreover, a rather senior post. The Kenyan wanted the Ugandan to help him to get a new job, and for this reason he spoke to him in Luganda, since this was the language most appropriate for conveying deference. The Kenyan's Luganda, in fact, was not particularly good, and so the Ugandan changed the conversation over into a third language, English. When, however, the time came for him actually to ask the favour outright, then the Kenyan again switched back to Luganda. In addition to being appropriately deferential, this also had the effect of stressing, since Luganda is a Bantu language, their ethnic affinity, in spite of their different nationalities.

The study of the way in which language is used in conversations of this and many other types is an important part of sociolinguistics. Sociolinguists have looked, as in the above example, at the way in which language can be used for manipulating relationships and achieving particular goals. They have also looked at rules for the conducting and interpretation of conversation, and at the way these may differ from society to society. We saw in Chapter 1 that it can often be embarrassing in English society to be together with someone and *not* talk to them. This is because language, in addition to being a means of communicating information, is an important means of establishing and maintaining relationships with other people. Young children have to learn not only the pronunciation, grammar and vocabulary of their language; they also have to learn how to use the language in conversational interaction in order to be able to establish social relationships and participate in two-way communication (rather than monologues).

One thing that children have to learn is the way in which conversations are structured. An obvious aspect of the structure of conversations is that they are based on the principle of turn-taking, and are organized in such a way as to ensure (in principle!) that only one speaker speaks at a time. In a conversation between two people, each speaker, obviously enough, takes a turn alternatively; but note that a speaker's 'turn' bestows not only the right but also the *obligation* to speak. If someone were reporting a conversation between Joan and Mary, they might say of one point 'and then Mary didn't say anything' in spite of the fact that at the moment in question neither Joan nor Mary said anything. The point is, of course, that it was Mary's 'turn', and that is why she is the one who is deemed to have remained silent.

There are also points in the structure of a conversation where it is possible, and points where it is not possible, to interrupt a speaker (an irritating fact about small children is that they do not always know the 'rules' about where those points are). And there are 'rules', too, about how and when one is allowed to introduce a new topic of conversation. There are even 'rules' about silence. It has been said that, in a conversation between two English speakers who are not close friends, a silence of longer than about four seconds is not allowed (which means that people become embarrassed if nothing is said after that time – they feel obliged to say *something*, even if it is only a remark about the weather). Many of these 'rules' can in fact be broken, but notice that people usually acknowledge the fact if they do break them. We say 'I'm sorry to interrupt', 'On a completely different topic', 'To go back to what we were talking about before', 'Just let me think about that for a minute', and so on.

We can also observe that conversations consist of structured *sequences* of different types of utterance. Clearly, a random sequence of utterances does not constitute a conversation. The structure of the sequences can sometimes, however, be quite complex. In most cases, for instance, conversations are organized so that questions are followed by answers:

> Q1: *Have you written to John yet?*
> A1: *No, not yet.*
> Q2: *Are you going to write?*
> A2: *Yes, eventually.*

However, it is perfectly possible for question and answer sequences to be embedded in one another:

> Q1: *Have you seen John yet?*

> Q2: *Is he back?*
> Q3: *Didn't you know?*
> A3: *No, I didn't.*
> A2: *He's back all right.*
> A1: *Well, I haven't seen him.*

Like questions, summonses are normally followed by answers:

> Bill, S1: *John!*
> John, A1: *Coming!*

Unlike question and answer sequences, however, they do not undergo embedding. The following is not a possible adult conversation:

> Bill, S1: *John!*
> John, S2: *Bill!*
> Bill, A2: *Yes?*
> John, A1: *Coming!*

The fact that a summons is normally followed by an answer may explain the rather odd fact, on the face of it, that in telephone conversations, it is usually the person who *answers* the telephone who speaks first. From a purely common-sense point of view, it could be said that more often than not the caller has a far better idea of who is going to answer the phone than the answerer has of who is calling. Nevertheless, the answerer speaks first because the ringing of the telephone functions as a summons which requires an answer, even if it is only 'hello'.

Conversations, then, are structured, rule-governed, non-random sequences of utterances. It is normally possible, at least for adults, as native speakers of a language and skilled conversationalists, to distinguish between coherent conversation-type sequences of utterances and random sequences. No one should have much trouble distinguishing between the following:

> (a) A: *Are you going on holiday this year?*
> B: *I haven't got any money.*

(b) A: *Are you going on holiday this year?*
   B: *My favourite colour is yellow.*

Ultimately, of course, our ability to do this depends on our knowledge of how the world is, but Labov has pointed out that there are a number of rules for the interpretation of conversational discourse that adults have mastered and that children do not always understand. One of these interpretive rules is relevant to the above example (a). The rule is this: if speaker A makes a request for information and speaker B's response is not related linguistically to the question (e.g. by ellipsis: 'No, I'm not (going on holiday this year)'), then that response must be interpreted as asserting that there exists a proposition, known to both A and B, which does make a connection, and from which an answer to A's question can be inferred. (The relevant proposition in example (a) is 'holidays cost money'.) This rule of interpretation is very strong. If we hear a sequence of utterances that seem, on the face of it, to be totally disconnected, such as:

A: *Are you going on holiday this year?*
B: *My aunt has just bought a bicycle.*

we nevertheless try to force an interpretation on the conversation by searching for a proposition that might make sense of it (such as, for example, that B and her aunt have for a long time been planning a cycling holiday). It is also of course possible for B to be mistaken in assuming that A shares knowledge of the proposition, or for A to deny the legitimacy of the proposition:

A: *Are you going on holiday this year?*
B: *I haven't got any money.*
A: *So what?*

The fact that rules for the interpretation of discourse exist can easily be demonstrated by showing what happens when they are broken. The American linguist Walt Wolfram, for instance, investigated people's reactions to questioning of the following sort:

A: *How old are you?*
B: *33.*
A: *How come?*

There is a rule of discourse interpretation which says that a *how come?* question involves an assertion that there exists a non-obvious proposition which is known to B, but which is not known to A. Wolfram interfered with the operation of this rule through asserting, by implication, that it was not obvious why B was 33. Reactions to his *how come?* question showed very clearly that something had gone wrong. Some people laughed, some were embarrassed, some made a joke of it – and others searched hard for some non-obvious proposition that would make sense of the interchange, such as 'I look older than 33 because . . .' or 'I'm still a student because . . .'.

Young children, of course, may have trouble with interpreting conversations, either because they are not familiar with a particular rule of interpretation, or because they are not yet aware of a particular proposition that is being asserted. The following would be a perfectly normal adult–child conversation:

Child: *Are we going on holiday this year?*
Adult: *We haven't got any money.*
Child: *But are we going on holiday?*

Wolfram demonstrated that adults are very well aware of the fact that children may have difficulties of this sort by getting his 6-year-old son Todd to carry out the same *how come?* questioning routine as above. In his case, relaxed and unembarrassed exchanges like the following occurred:

A: *How old are you?*
B: *33.*
A: *How come?*
B: *Because I was born in 1940.*

All societies, everywhere in the world, have rules about the way in which language should be used in social interaction. It is interesting to observe, however, that these rules may vary widely between one society and another. (The study of these rules, and of cross-cultural differences in communicative norms, is often known as the *ethnography of speaking*.) For instance, we noted above that it is normal amongst English speakers for the answerer to speak first in telephone conversations. There is nothing inevitable about this, though. Some people in Japan, for example, expect the caller to be the one to speak first. And there are other aspects of telephone behaviour, too, that can differ from one culture to another. Americans, for instance, find the following sort of telephone interchange quite normal:

> Answerer: *Hello.*
> Caller: *Is John there?*

The norm for French telephone conversations, as exemplified by the way in which children are taught to conduct such conversations, is very different, and goes more like this:

> Answerer: *Hello.*
> Caller: *Is that 123–4567?*
> A: *Yes.*
> C: *This is André here. I'm sorry to disturb you. Is Jean there?*

It is normal, that is, for callers to apologize for the intrusion, and to identify themselves. In American telephone conversations, callers are only really obliged to identify themselves if their intended addressee is not available:

> A: *No, I'm afraid John's out at the moment.*
> C: *OK. Please tell him Andy called.*

We also observed above that there are rules for the conduct of conversations which ensure that only one speaker speaks at a time. Studies in the ethnography of speaking, however, show that there are some cultures where this is not necessarily the case at all. In some Caribbean communities, as amongst certain groups of Black American adolescents, it is perfectly normal, at least in some situations, for everyone to talk at once. There are also many societies where it is quite normal for conversational silences to continue for much longer than four seconds. Some American Indian groups, such as the Navajo and Apache, have traditionally held to the norm that one does not speak unless one actually has something non-trivial to say.

It can readily be imagined that differences of this type between cultures can often lead, in cross-cultural communication, to misunderstanding and even hostility. Even when the cultures concerned are not very different, difficulties can arise. Northern Europeans, for instance, often feel that Americans are noisy and dominating simply because the norms for how loudly and how much one talks differ between the two areas. And where the cultural differences are greater, the misunderstandings can be greater, too. In Western Canada, for example, communication difficulties arise in interactions between English-speaking people of European origin and people who are speakers of a group of North American Indian languages known as Athabaskan. Differences between norms of language use between the two communities lead to misinterpretations and unfavourable stereotyping. One crucial difference between the two ethnic groups is that the Whites, like our two English people on the train, use language to establish social relations. They speak to people in order to get to know them, and in order to find out how they stand relative to each other. Among Athabaskan groups, on the other hand, speech is avoided if there is doubt about social relationships and about how one should behave. And quite lengthy silences, as with the Apache and Navajo (who are also Athabaskans), are readily tolerated. In interethnic communication there, therefore, English speakers start the conversation, because they want to set about establishing social relations and because the Athabaskans have remained silent (on account of their lack of certainty about the nature of the situation). The English speakers are therefore the ones who introduce the topic of the conversation. When there is a pause, they become uncomfortable about the silence well before the Athabaskans do, and therefore start speaking again. The result is a 'conversation' where English speakers hold the floor for most of the time and control what topics are talked about. The Athabaskans go away from the conversation thinking that English speakers are rude, dominating, superior, garrulous, smug and self-centred. The English speakers, on the other hand, find the Athabaskans rude, superior, surly, taciturn and withdrawn. In fact, hostility arises simply as a result of a failure by both parties to recognize that different groups of people have different norms concerning when and how language is to be used.

In fact, this can even happen, it seems, within the same society. The American sociolinguist Deborah Tannen has suggested that in many respects communication between men and women can be regarded as cross-cultural communication, at least in North America and Europe, though also, one suspects, elsewhere. She has suggested that men and women often fail to understand one another properly, and that such misunderstandings can lead to friction and tension in relationships. In fact, some Americans who have read her books on this subject have written to her to say that sociolinguistics has saved their marriages.

One aspect of communication that may cause problems of this type is the relationship between *directness* and *indirectness*. None of us say exactly what we think at all times – the world would be an even more antagonistic place than it already is if we did – and directness is something which speakers in all cultures tend to be very careful about. Direct questions, for example, can be particularly threatening, and in many English-speaking societies some direct questions are hardly ever asked – *How much money do you earn?* – while others will typically be accompanied by some overt recognition that this is a problematical linguistic activity: *How old are you – if I may ask? How much did you pay for it – if you don't mind telling me? Do you mind if I ask if you're married?*

Some cultures, however, seem to use direct questions much less frequently than others. The Australian sociolinguist Diana Eades has shown that some aboriginal Australians find direct questions so unusual, even if they are fluent or perhaps even monolingual speakers of English, that they do not understand them. She reports many conversations of the type:

> 'Was your wife still alive then?'
> 'Eh?'
> 'That would be when your wife was still alive.'
> 'Yes.'

Indirectness is used as a conversational strategy much more frequently in some cultures than others. In India, for example, people admiring a particular object belonging to someone else may find themselves being given it as a present. There may be many reasons for this – Indians are perhaps especially hospitable and generous – but one interpretation is that compliments may be perceived, by people who are sensitive to indirect hints being employed rather than direct requests, as if they were requests, whether this was actually intended or not. Even within Europe, the degree of use of indirectness may vary considerably from one culture to another. Northern Europeans living in rural Greece, for example, eventually learn to say not *Who's that person standing over there?* but *I've never seen that person who is standing over there before*. The point is that direct questions impose an obligation on interlocutors to provide an answer. Indirectness leaves them with a choice.

Indirectness, if interpreted correctly by cultural insiders or outsiders who have become familiar with the culture, can also help to avoid friction and antagonism. Western business people in Japan, for instance, have sometimes been confused by their Japanese counterparts responding to a proposal with 'yes' when, as it later turns out, they were actually not in favour. If they had been in favour, then they would have responded in a much more emphatically favourable way. Tannen similarly reports that when a young Greek woman who was still living with her parents was asked why she was not going to a party, after she had asked her father if she could go and he had replied 'yes,' she explained that her father had not really wanted her to go because, if he had, he would have replied 'Yes, of course, go, and have a really wonderful time.'

It is possible that indirectness is used more in societies which are, or which have been until recently, heavily hierarchical in structure. If you want to avoid giving offence to people in authority over you, or if you want to avoid intimidating people lower in the social hierarchy than yourself, then indirectness may be an important strategy. It is possible, too, that the more frequent use by women in western societies of indirectness in conversation is due to the fact that women have traditionally had less power in these societies. In any case, it is precisely the use of indirectness to significantly different extents by men and women that Tannen points to as giving rise to gender-based differences in conversational style, and thus to misunderstandings. Men use indirectness significantly less often in stating their goals, beliefs and intentions than women do, and therefore run the risk of being perceived by women as being tactless, dominating and impolite. Because they use indirectness less, they are also not sufficiently sensitive to its use by women, and may well not realize when women have indirectly made a request or given an opinion. Women may therefore interpret men as being insensitive and self-absorbed. Women, on the other hand, because of their relative lack of directness, may be perceived by men as being evasive and indecisive. Because they are not sufficiently direct in what they say, moreover, they may be perceived by men as being uncommunicative. If misunderstandings are discussed after the event, men may say 'if that's what you think, why didn't you say so?' while women may reply 'I *did* say so, but you wouldn't listen!'

The British sociolinguist Jennifer Coates has suggested that men and women may differ conversationally in at least one other way also. At least in certain sections of British society, and at least in certain situations, men seem more inclined to prefer a more competitive kind of discourse, whereas women seem to feel on the whole more comfortable with a more cooperative style. Men, for example, may interrupt each other more, and take pleasure in argumentation and point-scoring.

Women, on the other hand, especially amongst groups of friends, may also go against the norm that only one person speaks at once, but in a rather different way. They may, as it were, interrupt another speaker to agree with her, or to supply corroboration, or to finish off what she was going to say for her, in a kind of supportive discourse style in which everyone combines to produce a form of joint monologue. This kind of difference can sometimes cause friction and misunderstanding, as when women participants in mixed-sex conversations complain that men are always interrupting them. Interestingly, Coates's research shows not only that men interrupt more than women, but also that women allow themselves to be interrupted more than men.

7. Language and Nation

In the previous chapter we noted two things about the socio-linguistic situation in Kampala. First, many individuals were either bilingual or multilingual – they could speak more than one language with a fair degree of proficiency. Secondly, this was a consequence of the fact that the society in which they lived was a multilingual society. Individual bilingualism of this type is not actually a *necessary* consequence of societal or national multilingualism: there are multilingual societies where many speakers never become bilingual to any significant degree – Switzerland, for example – and individual bilingualism, although much more widespread than the average English speaker might suspect, is by no means universal. But societal multilingualism is a very widespread phenomenon indeed. On a world scale, the multilingual situation that obtains in Uganda is the rule rather than the exception. The vast majority of the nation-states of the world have more than one language spoken indigenously within their frontiers. In some cases, such as Cameroon or Papua New Guinea, the number of languages may rise into the hundreds (although it is not easy, bearing in mind the difficulty we mentioned in Chapter 1 of defining what exactly a language is, to give an exact figure for areas like these).

Multilingual nations exist in all parts of the world, and very many examples could be cited. Difficulties only arise when one attempts to locate a country that is genuinely *mono*lingual. There appear to be very few. Even in Europe there are not many true examples, although we are accustomed to thinking of most European nations as monolingual. Most people would accept as true statements to the effect that Germans speak German, the French speak French, and so on. There are good reasons for this, but the reality of the matter is somewhat different. Nearly all European countries contain linguistic minorities – groups of speakers who have as their native variety a language other than that which is the official, dominant or major language in the country where they live. In some cases, where the minorities are relatively large, the nation-state usually has more than one official language. Examples are Belgium (Dutch – often known as Flemish in Belgium – and French) and Switzerland (German, French, Italian and Romansch).

Where the minority is smaller or less influential, the minority language or languages are unlikely to have official status, and their speakers, often out of sheer practical necessity, will tend to be bilingual. This last factor is what helps to give Europe its outwardly monolingual appearance. The overwhelming majority of French citizens *can* speak French, in spite of the fact that for a number of them it is a second language. The same sort of situation applies in the United Kingdom. The UK also gives every appearance of being monolingual, and visitors certainly need to learn no other language than English. Even this appearance, though, is somewhat deceptive. It is true that England has not had an indigenous linguistic minority since Cornish became extinct in the eighteenth or nineteenth century (accounts vary), but there are today sizeable groups of speakers of languages from the northern Indian subcontinent, such as Punjabi, living in the country (and there are also some grounds for arguing that the first language of many British people of West Indian origin is not English, although it is very similar – see Chapter 8). Welsh, moreover, is the first language of about a fifth of the population of Wales, while Scots Gaelic is spoken natively by about 70,000 people, largely in the West Highlands and Hebridean Islands of Scotland.

The extent of national multilingualism in Europe is illustrated in the following lists. The first list, which is not exhaustive, gives some idea of the extent to which dominant official national languages in particular countries are spoken by linguistic minorities elsewhere.

Language	Spoken by Linguistic Minority in:
German	Denmark, Belgium, France, Italy, Slovenia, Serbia, Romania, Russia, Ukraine, Kazakhstan, Hungary, Czechia, Poland
Turkish	Greece, Macedonia, Bulgaria, Romania, Moldova, Ukraine
Greek	Italy, Macedonia, Albania, Bulgaria Romania, Ukraine, Turkey
Albanian	Greece, Serbia, Macedonia, Italy
Hungarian	Austria, Serbia, Romania, Slovakia, Ukraine
Finnish	Sweden, Russia
Swedish	Finland
French	Italy
Polish	Lithuania, Czechia, Ukraine
Bulgarian	Romania, Greece, Ukraine
Danish	Germany
Dutch	France
Italian	Slovenia, Croatia
Ukrainian	Romania, Slovakia, Poland
Slovak	Hungary, Romania, Czechia
Czech	Poland, Romania, Slovakia
Slovene	Austria, Italy
Macedonian	Bulgaria, Greece, Albania

There are of course also a number of languages which are minority languages everywhere. Some of these are the following:

Language	Spoken in:
Sami (Lapp)	Norway, Sweden, Finland, Russia
Frisian	Germany, Netherlands
Basque	Spain, France
Catalan	Spain, France
Breton	France
Sorbian	Germany

Kashubian	Poland
Welsh	UK
Gaelic	UK

In addition to these, Yiddish and Romany (Gypsy) are quite widely spoken as minority languages in different parts of the continent. (The unusual case of Irish Gaelic will be discussed below.)

So, nearly all European nations are multilingual to a certain extent. Perhaps the most multilingual of all the countries in Europe, apart from Russia (most of which is in Asia anyway, of course), is Romania. The largest single group amongst the 24 million or so population have Rumanian as their mother tongue, but at least fourteen other languages are spoken natively in the country. Accurate numbers are not available, but Romany-speaking Gypsies constitute the largest minority with at least 10 per cent of the population, while the other large minorities are Hungarians, Germans, and Jews who speak Yiddish or, in some cases, Ladino (Judeo-Spanish). Other minority languages include Russian, Ukrainian, Serbian, Slovak, Tartar, Turkish, Bulgarian, Czech, Greek and Armenian.

Multilingualism on this scale clearly brings problems for governments and others concerned with national organizations of various kinds, and we shall discuss these problems below (p. 128ff.). Multilingualism on any scale, though, also brings with it problems for individuals and groups of individuals, especially those who are members of linguistic minorities. Unlike members of the majority-language group, they have to acquire proficiency in at least two languages before they can function as full members of the national community in which they live. Perhaps the biggest problem they have to face is educational. In some cases the problem will not, perhaps, be too severe, because the two languages involved may not be particularly different. Frisian children learning Dutch are presented with nothing like the difficulty of Sami children learning Swedish, since Frisian and Dutch are quite closely related languages. Or it may be that the educational policy of the country concerned is reasonably sophisticated linguistically, and the children learn to read and write in and are taught through the medium of their native language in the initial stages of their schooling, with the majority language being introduced later on. This approach has been adopted in many parts of Wales, as well as in Norway and other places. Its aims are that the children should acquire an ability to read, write and speak both their native language and the majority language.

In other cases the minority child may be faced with very considerable difficulty. This may occur where the two languages involved are not closely related and also, more importantly, where the educational policy of a particular nation-state is to discourage, or simply to ignore or not to encourage, minority languages. In extreme cases the minority language may be forbidden or disapproved of in school, and children punished or actively discouraged from using it there. This was formerly true both of Welsh in Wales and Gaelic in Scotland – at one time a law was in force that actually made the speaking of Gaelic illegal.

The effects of the attempted imposition of an alien standard such as English may be very serious. The attempted replacement of one language by another entails an effort to obliterate whole cultures; it is indicative of illogical ethnic attitudes ('The Welsh are inferior to the English'); and it can very seriously impair the educational progress of children who have to learn a new language before they can understand what the teacher is saying, let alone read and write.

This approach was for many years official policy in the United States, where it may have been at least partly responsible, together with the broader social attitudes to minority languages that went with it, for the widespread and rapid assimilation of minority language groups to the English-speaking majority. Today considerable provision *is* made for some minority groups, notably Spanish-speakers and Native American Indians, to be educated in their own language, and certain other steps have also been taken: public notices in New York City, for example, are posted in Spanish as well as

English, to cater for the large Puerto Rican community now living there. However, even the larger, more rural linguistic minorities such as those consisting of speakers of French (in the North-East and in Louisiana) and Pennsylvania Dutch (a form of German) are rapidly declining in size. In 1970, the ten largest linguistic minorities in the US were as follows:

Spanish	7.9 million	Yiddish	1.5 million
German	6.2	Norwegian	0.6
Italian	4.0	Swedish	0.6
French	2.6	Slovak	0.5
Polish	2.3	Hungarian	0.5

In all, about 34 million Americans currently have a mother-tongue other than English.

Happily, the English-only approach and the attitude associated with it have almost disappeared from the educational scene in the United Kingdom too, although there are many Welsh and Gaelic speakers who are very unhappy about the status of their languages. Gaelic has been allowed in schools in Gaelic-speaking Scottish areas since 1918, although it was not really until 1958 that it began to be used extensively as a medium of instruction, and then mainly for younger children in primary schools. For most older children, particularly in secondary schools, English is still the normal medium, partly as a consequence of the centralization of secondary education, which has meant that many Gaelic speakers go to schools where there are also large numbers of non-Gaelic-speaking children.

The position of Welsh in the UK is considerably more healthy than that of Gaelic. It has far more speakers, and fairly considerable amounts of time are given to radio and TV broadcasts in Welsh (although not as much as some would like). As in the case of Gaelic, the effects of the older educational approach linger on. Many older people today, while being fluent speakers of Welsh, have never learned to write it. They have to write even the most intimate of letters in a foreign language, English, and very often find it difficult to read Standard Welsh. Today the situation is much improved, and especially since the early 1930s there has been a change in emphasis. At around that time Welsh began to be taught seriously in many primary schools in Welsh-speaking areas, although its role in secondary schools was very minor. Subsequently, in 1953, a report was published which received Ministry of Education approval: it suggested that all children in Wales should be taught both Welsh and English. This bilingual policy has been widely adopted today, although the actual situation is rather complex since policy is decided on an area basis by local education authorities. Generally, however, one can say that in most parts of Wales, whether anglicized or not, one can find some schools at both primary and secondary level where Welsh is taught only as a subject, others where it is used as a medium along with English, and others where Welsh is the only medium and English is taught as a subject. Another interesting development is the institution of nursery schools which are solely Welsh-speaking but to which many English-speaking parents are sending their children in order that they should grow up bilingual. Like, apparently, many Irish people, some of these Welsh parents feel that by adopting the English language they or their ancestors have in some way been untrue to their cultural traditions, and hope that their children will be able to rectify this state of affairs. The schools appear to work very well, and suggest that there may well be an increase in the number of fluent Welsh speakers in the next generation. Indeed, figures from the 1981 census suggest that the decline in the number of Welsh speakers may have now halted, and is possibly even being reversed. Nevertheless, the future of the Celtic languages in Britain is still very precarious. There was a decline in the number of Gaelic speakers in Scotland from 136,000 in 1831 to 81,000 in 1931, and a decline in the number of Welsh speakers over the same period from 902,000 to 656,000.

The teaching of minority languages in this way is obviously of benefit to minority-group children, not only in the learning of reading and writing but in other subjects as well. It also has the effect of recognizing the child's social and cultural identity and integrity and encourages the development and growth of minority cultures. At the same time it does not deny the child access to the majority language, which is likely to be essential for upward social mobility. Gaelic and Welsh speakers who know English can more readily function as members of the wider national community, if they wish to.

The position of other European minority languages in education varies considerably. Those languages, like German, which are majority languages elsewhere have a clear practical advantage over languages like Gaelic and Sami (Lapp) for which there is a scarcity of teaching materials and reading matter. On the other hand, they may be at a political disadvantage. German receives very little encouragement in France, while Macedonian in Greece and German in Romania are actually discouraged. (We shall discuss this political point below.) Frisian is given some encouragement in the Netherlands, while some attempts have been made to promote Sami education in Scandinavia.

Where language is a defining characteristic (see p. 41) of a minority ethnic group wanting independence, particularly where other (for example physical) characteristics are not significant (as in the case of Welsh), linguistic factors are likely to play an important role in any separatist movement they might undertake. This is partly in response to practical problems, such as education, but mainly a result of the fact that language, as we have already seen (p. 11), acts as an important symbol of group consciousness and solidarity. The extent to which this is true is revealed in the part played by linguistic groupings in the development of new independent nations in Europe after the breakdown of the older, multilingual empires. As national consciousness grew, languages like Finnish and several others developed a literature, underwent standardization, and emerged as national languages of fairly monoglot areas when independence was achieved.

The rapid increase in the number of independent European nation-states in the past hundred years or so has therefore been paralleled by a rapid growth in the number of autonomous, national and official languages. During the nineteenth century the number rose from sixteen to thirty, and since that time has risen to over fifty. It is interesting to plot some of the stages of this development, particularly since the movement has not been entirely in one direction. During the Middle Ages, for example, some languages – like Provençal and Arabic – ceased to function (the latter in Europe alone) as standardized official languages, while others – like English and Norwegian – became submerged, only to reappear later. By 1800, the following had come to be operating as national languages in Europe (excluding Russia): Icelandic, Swedish, Danish, German, Dutch, English, French, Spanish, Portuguese, Italian, Polish, Hungarian, Greek and Turkish. By 1900 the following had also made an appearance (or reappearance) as standardized national, official or written languages: Norwegian, Finnish, Welsh, Rumanian, and the Slav languages Czech, Slovak, Slovene, Serbo–Croat and Bulgarian. And during the rest of this century Irish Gaelic, Scots Gaelic, Breton, Catalan, Romansch, Macedonian, Albanian and Basque have all undergone standardization, revival or expansion.

The problems of the multilingual situation for the individual can be overcome or minimized either through political independence or semi-independence, or, less drastically, through adequate educational programmes and policies. What, however, of the problems of multilingualism for national governments? Many governments regard as a problem the fact that language can act as a focus of discontent for minorities wanting more power, independence, or annexation by a neighbouring state. Where goverments do not regard this as threatening or undesirable, they may well regard linguistic minorities benevolently (or simply ignore them). It does not appear, for example, that the British government is seriously concerned about Gaelic speakers. Scandinavian governments, similarly, for the most part believe they have nothing to fear from the Sami. The government of the Republic of Ireland, too, gives active support to the minority language (something between 1 and 3 per cent of the population speak Irish natively), and have made it a compulsory subject in schools. This, of course, is because Irish was formerly the language of all the Irish and as such symbolizes national culture and identity rather than dissidence of any kind.

On the other hand, in cases where governments regard linguistic minorities as potentially 'subversive', they may react very differently. Their fears, from their own point of view, may often be justified: language loyalty can be a powerful weapon, and has often been manipulated to political advantage. In many cases a repressed or discouraged minority language is also the language of a possibly antagonistic neighbouring state – this has been true of Macedonian in Greece, Slovenian in Italy, and German in France and Italy – and the fear is that language loyalty may prove to be stronger than national loyalty. In other cases disfavoured minority languages may simply have acted as catalysts of discontent, because minority groups have had one additional reason to be dissatisfied with their lot.

One language which has had a history of oppression for reasons of this kind is Catalan. Catalan is a Romance language which is about as closely related to French as it is to Spanish. It has approximately seven million speakers in Spain – in Catalonia, Valencia and the Balearic Islands – as well as about 250,000 in Roussillon in France, and a very small group in Sardinia. It is also one of the two official languages of Andorra (the other is French). It was the official, administrative written language in Catalonia until that area was annexed by Castile at the beginning of the eighteenth century. Subsequently, in 1768, Spanish was introduced by government decree into formerly Catalan schools, and then in 1856 a law was passed which stated that all political documents and legal contracts were to be in Spanish. Liberalization of this policy took place under the Spanish Republic, from 1931 to 1939. Catalan-speaking children were taught in Catalan, while provision was made for Spanish-speaking children in the Catalan area to begin their education in Spanish, and at the age of ten both groups started to learn the other language as well. However, under the Franco government Catalan was once again banned completely from schools, and chairs of Catalan language and literature at the University of Barcelona were abolished. Catalan text books disappeared, and Catalan children again had to begin and complete their education in Spanish. Supporters of Catalan claimed that the Franco government was fundamentally 'Castilian nationalist' in character, and clearly it was concerned about what it regarded as separatist tendencies. Language is a signal of group identity, and anybody attempting to create a unified nation-state, particularly of the corporate Franco type, will find any signalling of a *different* identity undesirable or dangerous. Linguistic subjugation (or unification, depending on one's point of view) is therefore an important strategy in implementing political subjugation (or unification).

In the later years of the Franco régime the situation of Catalan was somewhat relaxed. Many books became available and there were two children's comics and one magazine in the language. There were still, however, no newspapers, and broadcasting time was very limited indeed. Most significant of all was that Catalan remained forbidden in the schools. This meant that upon arriving in school for the first time, Catalan children were unable to understand what the teacher was saying – for the first few weeks at least – and that they grew up unable to read and write in their own language, unless their parents took the trouble to teach them these skills at home. The extent of the linguistic problem involved is partly revealed by the following passage in Catalan, and its Spanish translation.

Catalan:

Maigret escolta distret, tot pensant que la meitat de Paris està de vacances i que la resta, en aquesta hora, beu begudes fresques a les tauletes de les terrasses. Quina comtessa? Ah si! L'home trist s'explica. Una senyora que ha tingut més d'un revés de fortuna i que ha obert un saló de bridge al carrer Pyramides. Una dona ben bonica. Es nota que el pobre home n'està enamorat. – Avui, a les quatre, he agafat un bitllet de mil de la caixa dels amos.

Spanish:

Maigret escucha distraidemente, pensando que medio Paris está de vacaciones y que el resto a estas horas estará tomando refrescos en las

mesitas de las terrazas. Que condesa? Ah, si! El hombre triste s'explica.
Una señora que ha sufrido más de un contratiempo y que abrió un
salón de bridge en la calle Pirámides. Una mujer muy guapa. Se
conoce que el pobre hombre está enamorado. – Hoy, a las cuatro, he
cogido un billete de mil de la caja de los dueños.

English:

'Maigret only half listens, thinking that half Paris will be on
holiday and that the rest, at this hour, will be drinking cool drinks
outside at small café-tables on the pavement. Which countess? Ah
yes! The sad man explains. A lady who has had more than one set-
back and who has opened a bridge-club on Pyramides Street. A
rather pretty woman. It is apparent that the poor man is in love with
her. "Today, at four o'clock, I took a thousand-franc note from the
bosses' till."'

However, since the democratization of Spain in the 1970s, the
situation has changed very significantly. The position of Catalan has greatly improved and very many of the above problems, therefore, have to a great extent disappeared. Catalan
has returned to the domains, in the media and in education,
from which it had been banished.

The same sort of motives that we have ascribed to the
former Spanish government were clearly also present in the
case of the British government which prohibited Scots Gaelic
in the aftermath of the 1745 rebellion. Similar factors influenced the actions of those Greek governments which carried
out a policy of hellenization in northern Greece by proscribing
the usage of Macedonian in that area.

The activities of governments having to do with language
can be described as instances of *language planning*. In very
many cases activities of this kind, unlike many of those we
have just described, can be regarded as both necessary and
commendable – for example in countries which are faced with
the problem of having to select a national language or languages and, subsequently, of developing and standardizing it.
We have already noted some of the problems resulting from
multilingualism in Europe. In many areas of the world the
problems are considerably more complex. Sub-Saharan
Africa, for example, is a very multilingual area where lan-

guage problems have been exacerbated because colonial powers drew national frontiers without regard for the geographical distribution of ethnic or linguistic groups.

However, communication problems in areas like these are not necessarily so serious as one might think. In our Kampala example, for instance (p. 108), we saw that people were able to communicate with each other quite easily, in spite of the fact that they did not know each other's languages, because they were also familiar with other languages like Luganda, Swahili and English: each of these three languages was capable of functioning as a *lingua franca*. A *lingua franca* is a language which is used as a means of communication among people who have no native language in common. Some of the languages which are used in this way in Africa, like English and French, are not indigenous to the area in question and are often learned through formal education. Many African lingua francas, though, are indigenous, and may have come to be used as such because of the political dominance of their native speakers, like Luganda, or because they were the language of prominent traders in the area, like Swahili. In West Africa one of the most important lingua francas which is still used for predominantly trading purposes is Hausa. Hausa is an Afro-Asiatic language spoken originally in the region of Lake Chad in north-central Africa, but it has become so widely known that it is used for trading and other purposes by many millions of speakers in areas such as Ghana, Nigeria and Dahomey. Many languages have spread as lingua francas in the same kind of way, only to contract again later for reasons of economics or politics. Greek, for example, became a lingua franca in the ancient world as a result, initially, of Alexander's military conquests, and was at one time used widely from Turkey to Portugal. Latin was later used as a lingua franca in the western world, mainly as a result of the expansion of the Roman empire, and later survived as such, in spite of the fact that it had no native speakers, for many centuries. The original 'lingua franca' from which the term (which actually means 'French language') is derived, was a form of Provençal that was used as a lingua franca by the multilingual crusaders.

When governments are presented with the problem, as many 'new' nations have been, of selecting a national language or languages, lingua francas of this type are obviously very useful. There are clear advantages to be gained from the selection of a language which many people already understand. In some cases, though, complications may arise because competing or alternative lingua francas are available. In India, Hindi is used as a lingua franca in much of the northern part of the country. It has the advantage of being an indigenous rather than an originally colonial language, like English, but it also has the disadvantage of benefiting native speakers to the detriment of others who have to learn it as a second language. English, on the other hand, operates as a lingua franca throughout the country, but tends to be used only by relatively educated speakers; an educated Bengali speaker would probably communicate in English with an educated Tamil speaker if, as is likely, neither knew the other's first language.

A similar problem of competing lingua francas occurred in Malaysia. The Federation of Malaysia was formed in 1963 with a population of only ten million, but with a linguistic situation that was very complex. In Malaya itself Malay is the native language of perhaps 30 per cent of the population, although it has several different forms, including the Standard Malay of the educated urban élite; colloquial Malay, which has many different dialectal variants; and 'bazaar Malay', which is widely used as a trading lingua franca. Another 30 per cent speak one of twelve different Chinese languages, the four most widely used being Cantonese, Hokkien, Hakka and Tiechiu. (In each urban Chinese community one of these normally functions as a lingua franca.) Then roughly 10 per cent speak various Indian languages, mainly Tamil, but also other Dravidian languages such as Telugu and Malayalam, and the Indo-European Punjabi; in addition to these, many of the Eurasian community speak a form of Portuguese, while English is a lingua franca for many of the educated. Thai and several 'aboriginal' languages are also spoken. The sociolinguistic picture is further complicated by the languages which are used as the medium of instruction in schools. Malay, Tamil and English are all used in this way, but so is Mandarin Chinese, which is not one of the main varieties of Chinese spoken natively in the country, and Arabic.

Elsewhere, in those parts of the country that formerly constituted British North Borneo, many different languages are spoken which are related to Malay, as well as some that are related to certain of the languages of the Philippines, and also Chinese. There is therefore clearly a problem in Malaysia as to which language should be selected to act as the national language. Malay is the most widely understood lingua franca, but Malays are politically dominant in the country and attempts to make Malay the sole official language might well cause some resentment among the Chinese and Indians. It would also entail a shortage of textbooks, many of which are now in English, and a certain amount of loss of international contacts. English on the other hand cannot be claimed to be in any sense a national language, but it is the most popular educational medium, for what are largely economic reasons. Success in the professions in Malaysia appears to require ability in English, while Malay is required for the Civil Service, and Chinese for business. The problem has as yet not really been solved, but while group identity plays an important part in maintaining language loyalty towards languages like Tamil, these community languages appear to be gradually ceding in importance to Malay (for reasons of national loyalty) and to English (for reasons of international economics) in more official functions and circumstances. Government policy appears to be in the direction of strengthening both Malay and English.

A further solution has sometimes been advocated for problems of multilingualism – that an artificial language such as Esperanto should be adopted as a lingua franca. At present it seems unlikely that any nation-state will adopt Esperanto as its official language because of the practical problems involved, and also because, being a neutral language, it is not national in any way. However, supporters of Esperanto are much more concerned to see it used as a world-wide lingua franca in order to solve problems of *international multilingualism*. In multilingual, multi-national communities, like the European Union, disputes can often arise as to which language or languages are to be used officially. Advocates of Esperanto would suggest that, if it were made the official language of the EU, disputes of this kind would not arise. Unlike English or French, Esperanto is the native language of no one, and therefore gives nobody an unfair advantage, just as English in India is in many ways a fairer choice as a lingua franca than Hindi. This argument would probably not hold, however, for larger international organizations like the United Nations. This is because Esperanto, although it is easier to learn than natural languages, is quite clearly a *European*-type language, and would therefore benefit native speakers of languages originally from this area. In any case, there are as yet no real signs of Esperanto, or any other similar language, making very great headway on the international scene.

Often the role of a national government does not stop at selecting a national language. Once selected, the language may have to be established, developed and standardized. The government, for example, may play a part in developing a suitable orthography, or in deciding whether a particular dialect of the language or some set of compromise forms should be selected. English, of course, developed a standard variety by relatively 'natural' means, over the centuries, out of a kind of consensus, due to various social factors. For many 'newer' countries, though, the development of a standard language has had to take place fairly rapidly, and government intervention has therefore been necessary. Standardization, it is argued, is necessary in order to facilitate communications, to make possible the establishment of an agreed orthography, and to provide a uniform form for school books. (It is, of course, an open question as to how much, if any, standardization is really required. It can be argued quite reasonably that there is no real point in standardizing to the extent where, as is often the case in English-speaking communities, children spend many hours learning to spell in an *exactly* uniform manner, where any spelling mistake is the subject of opprobrium or ridicule, and where deviations from the standard are interpreted as incontrovertible evidence of ignorance.)

One of the most interesting examples of government activity in the field of language planning and language standardization is provided by modern Norway. There are in Norway today two official standard Norwegian languages. On the face of it this is a rather strange state of affairs for a country of four million or so inhabitants. The two standards are known as Nynorsk ('new Norwegian') and Bokmål ('book language') – neither of them particularly apt names – and both have equal official status. (In other words the relationship is not a diglossic one in the sense of Chapter 5.) Bokmål is the language of the national press (although some newspapers include articles in Nynorsk), of a majority of books, particularly translations, and of a majority of schoolchildren, as the medium of education. Nynorsk is used in some of the local press, particularly in the west of the country; it is the school language of about 20 per cent of children; and it is used in much poetry and literature, particularly in works with a rural background. All official documents are in both standards; children have to learn to read and write both; and both are extensively used in radio and television. In each area local councils decide which variety is to be used in public notices, and the standard to be used in each school district is also decided by democratic procedures.

Linguistically speaking the two are very similar, and they are totally mutually comprehensible. The dichotomy, moreover, applies much more to the written standard languages than to the spoken language. Most people speak rural dialects or nonstandard urban dialects, although western dialects do tend to resemble Nynorsk more closely, and some eastern dialects are more similar to Bokmål. Perhaps sociolinguistically more interesting than the differences *between* the two languages, however, are the differences *within* them. In both Bokmål and Nynorsk there are variants (alternative pronunciations and grammatical constructions) which are known as *radical* and *conservative*. In the case of Bokmål, right-wing newspapers tend to use conservative forms, and left-wing papers radical forms. It is also often possible to make an intelligent guess about educated speakers' politics from the forms they use. This involvement of language with politics, in a rather unusually overt form, means that few Norwegians are very objective about the linguistic situation in their country, and that the 'language question' is often very hotly debated indeed. The heat of the argument can be judged from the fact that in 1955 a weather-forecaster on the Norwegian radio became known as the 'abominable snowman' and was actually dismissed because he refused to say *snø* (a radical Bokmål form) 'snow' instead of *sne* (a conservative form).

This Norwegian situation is clearly unusual, and, many Norwegians would say, a very awkward one, because it is expensive in a country with such a small population to print school books and official documents in both languages, and time-consuming for schools to have to teach both. In my own view it is in many ways a very good situation, since it means that far more Norwegians than would otherwise be the case are able to learn to read and, if they wish, write, speak and express themselves in a standard language that closely resembles their own native variety (dialectal variation being quite considerable in Norway).

It is interesting to trace the development of this situation because, although it is unique in Europe, it is nonetheless indicative of the type of language-planning activity in which governments can participate. Norway was ruled by Denmark from the fifteenth century until 1814. During this time the only official language was Danish, with the result that Norwegian dialects became heteronomous with respect to standard Danish. This was only possible, of course, because Danish resembled Norwegian quite closely. When independence from Denmark was won in 1814 there was therefore no specifically Norwegian standard language. A small number of immigrants actually spoke Danish, which was also used in the theatre, while the formal language of native government officials was in effect Danish with a Norwegian pronunciation. This was also how reading was taught in schools. The informal speech of upper-class speakers was a kind of compromise between this and local varieties: it was a fairly uniform kind of Danish-influenced Norwegian. Lower-class speakers in towns spoke Norwegian dialects perhaps somewhat influenced by Danish, whereas peasants and farmers spoke rural Norwegian dialects.

Two distinct responses were made to growing feelings in the country in favour of establishing a national Norwegian language. One strategy was to revise Danish gradually in the direction of the language of those upper-class urban people who spoke the Danish-influenced Norwegian. This Dano-Norwegian came to be known as Riksmål ('state language'), and was the forerunner of Bokmål. The other response was advocated by Ivar Aasen, a school teacher who had made an extensive study of Norwegian dialects. He advocated a more revolutionary approach, and devised a language of his own based on his dialect studies. The language was based on those rural dialects, mainly those of the West, which Aasen thought to be least 'contaminated' by Danish, and was called Landsmål ('language of the country'), which later became Nynorsk. In 1885, in response to various nationalist sentiments, Landsmål was made an official language on a par with Danish (or Riksmål). The government, however, did not feel free to abolish Dano-Norwegian because this was still the language of the influential urban élite. In fact, the position of Dano-Norwegian was strengthened when teachers were instructed, in 1887, not to teach the reading pronunciation of Danish but rather the colloquial standard, the modified Dano-Norwegian Riksmål. These two acts were the government's first involvement in language planning.

The origin of the conservative and radical forms in the two official languages today lies in the desire of successive governments to establish one national language instead of two without actually abolishing either of them. Rather the desire has been to reform the two gradually towards each other. For example, Norwegian dialects, including those of the urban working-class, have three genders for nouns (masculine, feminine and neuter), whereas Dano-Norwegian, subsequently Riksmål, had, like Danish, only two (common and neuter). This meant that Riksmål had identical forms for the definite article (which in Norwegian is placed after the noun) for masculine and feminine words: *mann* 'man', *ko* 'cow'; *mannen* 'the man', *koen* 'the cow'. Landsmål had distinct forms: *kui* 'the cow'. In 1917 the government introduced an official reform, one of the effects of which was to achieve a compromise between the two languages on this (and other) points. In Landsmål the form of the feminine definite article was to be changed from *-i* to *-a* to bring it into line with eastern dialects, while in Riksmål the feminine form *-a* was introduced obligatorily for some words, particularly words with rural associations, like *cow*, and optionally for others. This meant that 'the cow' was now *kua* in both languages. ('Obligatory' here means obligatory in school textbooks and in schoolchildren's writing.) As a result of this reform the feminine definite article used in conjunction with some nouns in Bokmål is considered to be a radical form, the masculine (or common) article a conservative form.

The next important development in government language planning was the 1938 reform, which was based on the report of a committee whose mandate was 'to bring the two languages closer together with respect to spelling, word-forms, and inflections, on the basis of the Norwegian folk language'. They were thus specifically instructed *not* to model the standard languages on the speech of the educated upper classes, an unusual and important step in the history of language standardization. Major changes that were to be made in Bokmål schoolbooks were the introduction of diphthongs for monophthongs in many words, as in Nynorsk and many dialects:

> *øst* > *aust* 'east' cf. Danish *øst*
> *sten* > *stein* 'stone' cf. Danish *sten*

and a change in the past tense endings of verbs from *-et* to *-a*, again as in many lower-prestige eastern dialects, rural dialects, and Nynorsk:

vaknet > *vakna* 'woke up'

The implementation of these reforms was delayed by the Second World War, but after the war schoolbooks began to be issued in the new standards. The changes in Bokmål provoked angry reactions on the part of upper-class speakers, and many middle-class speakers in the East. Many parents, particularly in Oslo, felt these new forms to be vulgar, and objected to the fact that the same forms they had tried to 'correct' in their children's speech were now actually appearing in print. During the early 1950s, therefore, large business concerns and conservative politicians financed widespread campaigns against the reforms. Tremendous controversy ensued, and it was against this background that the 'abominable snowman' incident took place.

In spite of this opposition, a new Language Commission was set up with the same mandate as the committee that had produced the 1938 report, in order to supervise schoolbook norms for the two languages. (Right-wingers regarded the commission as representing the 'legalization of vulgarity', left-wingers a 'victory for democracy'.) In 1959 these schoolbook norms were published, and turned out to be basically the same as the 1938 forms, although not so radical. As a result of their recommendations there are now three different types of form in schoolbooks, in both Bokmål and Nynorsk: *obligatory* forms (only one possibility permitted); *alternative* forms (two possibilities permitted); and *optional* forms (not permitted in print, but children can use them in their own writing). Speakers and writers of the two Norwegians therefore have a considerable amount of choice open to them, in many ways a very good thing.

Specific proposals made by the commission were that the feminine definite article in Bokmål should be obligatory with a rather smaller number of nouns; the number of past-tense forms where -*a* was obligatory was sharply reduced and -*a* and -*et* were made alternatives; and diphthongs became obligatory in fewer words. A diphthong, for example, is obligatory in *sein* 'late' (although conservative newspapers still write *sen*); an alternative in *beisk/besk* 'bitter'; an optional form in (*eid*)/*ed* 'oath'; and a monophthong is obligatory in *en* 'one' (*ein* is Nynorsk only). (Similarly, and more amusingly, *daud* 'dead' is all right for animals, but *død* should be used of people.) The following is useful for diagnosing the provenance of written publications in Bokmål:

	'the book'	'delayed'
political right	*boken*	*forsinket*
political left	*boka*	*forsinket*
many schoolbooks	*boka*	*forsinka*

The two sentences following illustrate in greater detail the relationship between the two languages, as well as some of the differences within them. (Not all the forms used here are actually allowed in the schoolbook norms, but most of them can be found in printed works of various kinds. Some of the 'radical' forms are much more 'radical' than others, and no attempt has been made to preserve stylistic consistency in any of the versions.)

A final footnote on the Norwegian linguistic scene: Norway actually has two names in Norwegian, *Noreg* in Nynorsk, and *Norge* in Bokmål.

We saw that, under Danish rule, Norwegian dialects became heteronomous with respect to Danish – they were regarded as dialects of Danish. Now they are not – they are regarded as dialects of Norwegian, because Norwegian has acquired autonomy as an independent language. As we saw in Chapter 1, the difference between a language and a dialect is often a political one. As the Norwegian example makes clear, because autonomy is a cultural phenomenon, it can be lost or acquired. Norwegian used to be a dialect; now it is a language. Afrikaans used to be a dialect of Dutch; now it is not. The same is true of Macedonian, which used to be regarded as consisting of dialects of Bulgarian but which is now regarded, by Macedonians if not by Bulgarians, as a separate language.

Scots, on the other hand, was formerly a language in its own right, but is now widely regarded as heteronomous to

This interlinear example compares the same passage in six Norwegian written norms.

Part 1

	When	she	awoke	under	the	raw-cold	winter clouds	even	more	the morning	after,	felt
Conservative Nynorsk:	Då	ho	vakna	under	dei	råkalde	vinterskyene	endå	meir	morgonen	etter,	kjendest
Moderate Nynorsk:	Da	ho	vakna	under	dei	råkalde	vinterskyene	enda	meir	morgonen	etter,	kjendest
Radical Nynorsk:	Da	ho	vakna	under	dei	råkalde	vinterskyene	enda	meir	morgonen	etter,	kjendest
Radical Bokmål:	Da	hun	våknet (vaknet)	under	de	råkalde	vinterskyene	enda	mer	morgenen	etter,	føltes
Moderate Bokmål:	Da	hun	våknet	under	de	råkalde	vinterskyene	enda	mer	morgenen	etter,	føltes
Conservative Bokmål:	Da	hun	våknet	under	de	råkalde	vinterskyer	enda	mer	morgenen	etter,	føltes
(literal translation)	When	she	awoke	under	the	raw-cold	winter clouds	even	more	the morning	after,	felt

Part 2

	the town	dreary
Cons. Nn.:	byen	troysteslaus
Mod. Nn.:	byen	troysteslaus
Rad. Nn.:	byen	trøsteslaus
Rad. Bm.:	byen	trøsteslaus
Mod. Bm.:	byen	trøstesløs
Cons. Bm.:	byen	trøstesløs

Part 3

	than	any	time	before.	It was	because	she	had
Cons. Nn.:	enn	noken	gong	før	Det var	av di	ho	hadde
Mod. Nn.:	enn	noken	gong	før	Det var	fordi	ho	hadde
Rad. Nn.:	enn	noen	gong	før	Det var	fordi	ho	hadde
Rad. Bm.:	enn	noen	gang	før	Det var	fordi	hun	hadde
Mod. Bm.:	enn	noen	gang	før	Det var	fordi	hun	hadde
Cons. Bm.:	enn	noen	gang	før	Det var	fordi	hun	hadde
	than	any	time	before.	It	was	because	she	had

	another world	to	compare	it	with:	that	world	which
Cons. Nn.:			*samanlikna*	*honom*			*verdi*	*som*
Mod. Nn.:			*samanlikna*	*han*			*verda*	*som*
Rad. Nn.:	*ei anna verd*	*å*	*samanlikne*	*han*	*med:*	*den*	*verda*	*som*
Rad. Bm.:	*ei anna verd*	*å*	*sammenlikne*	*den*	*med:*	*den*	*verda*	*som*
Mod. Bm.:	*en annen verden*		*sammenligne*	*den*			*verden*	
Cons. Bm.:	*en annen verden*		*sammenligne*	*den*			*verden*	

	lived	within	him,	the	fine	cities	which	shone	out
Cons. Nn.:			*honom,*			*storbyane*	*som*	*lyste*	*ut*
Mod. Nn.:			*han,*			*storbyene*	*som*	*lyste*	*ut*
Rad. Nn.:	*budde*	*inne*	*i han,*	*dei*	*vakre*	*storbyane*	*som*		
Rad. Bm.:	*budde*	*inne*	*i han,*	*de*	*vakre*	*storbyene*	*som*		
Mod. Bm.:	*bodde*	*inne*	*ham,*			*storbyene*			
Cons. Bm.:	*bodde*	*inne*	*ham,*			*storbyer*			

	from	his	eyes
Cons. Nn.:	*or*	*augo*	*hans.*
Mod. Nn.:	*av*	*auga*	*hans.*
Rad. Nn.:	*av*	*auga*	*hans.*
Rad. Bm.:	*av*	*øyene*	*hans.*
Mod. Bm.:	*av*	*øynene*	*hans.*
Cons. Bm.:	*av*	*hans*	*øyne.*

from his eyes ('eyes-the his' in all except Cons. Bm.).

English. Similarly, Provençal and Low German, formerly autonomous, are now generally regarded as dialects of French and German, respectively. Autonomy can also be disputed. Because Catalan was part of the same dialect continuum as Spanish, it was possible for the Franco regime to suggest that it was 'really' a dialect of Spanish. Similarly, earlier in this chapter I used the term Serbo-Croat. In former Yugoslavia, given the desire of the government to stress national unity, it was usual, as we saw in Chapter 3, to regard Serbo-Croat as a single language with two somewhat different norms, not unlike British and American English. Since the early 1990s, now that Croatia has become a separate nation, it has become official policy to regard Serbian and Croatian as separate – although mutually intelligible – languages, like Norwegian and Danish. Notice that there can be no linguistic answer to whether Serbian and Croatian are one language or two. The answer is a political and cultural one.

There are many other such political, sociolinguistic questions in modern Europe. Is Macedonian really a language? Is there a Bosnian language which is distinct from Croatian and Serbian? Are Moldovan and Rumanian the same language or not? Are Flemish and Dutch one language or two? Is Corsican a dialect of Italian or not? Is Swiss German actually a separate language? Because of the discreteness and continuity problem, there is no way we can answer these questions on purely linguistic grounds. Ironically, it seems that it is only linguists who fully understand the extent to which these questions are not linguistic questions. The fact is that most European languages are 'languages by extension' (in German, *Ausbau* languages). They consist of standard varieties which have been *superposed* over continua of dialects which, for social and historical reasons, have become heteronomous to them. There are also, however, languages of which this is not true. We can call Basque a 'language by distance' (in German, *Abstand* language) because it is linguistically so different from all other languages that its status as an independent language cannot be disputed.

8. Language and Geography

We saw in Chapter 2 that there is a relationship in Britain between social dialects and geographical dialects such that regional linguistic differentiation is greatest at the level of varieties most unlike Standard English. This is true in many other countries also. The social and linguistic reasons for the development of regional differences of this type are complex, and by no means completely understood. They are clearly the result of language changing in different ways in different places, but the actual process of linguistic change is something we have still to learn much about.

Earlier on in this book, we briefly discussed the importance, in the development of regional dialects, of geographical features such as barriers and distance. When a linguistic innovation – a new word, a new pronunciation, a new usage – occurs at a particular place, it may subsequently spread to other areas, particularly those nearest to it, so long as no serious barriers to communication intervene. If an innovation started in London, we would expect to find that it later began to be used in Cambridge before it found its way into the speech of Carlisle. It might, though, take considerably longer to reach Belfast, because of the Irish Sea. This is an obvious point, and one that does not apply only to language. All technological and behavioural innovations are subject to the same processes. When mini-skirts were becoming fashionable in the 1960s studies showed that girls were generally wearing their skirts shorter in London than they were in Newcastle, where, in turn, they were shorter than those worn in Edinburgh.

The social and geographical pressures involved in the diffusion of linguistic innovations are of course a good deal more complex than those associated with fashions. It is possible, however, to demonstrate in a broad kind of way that similar factors are at work. A good example of a linguistic innovation which has been subject to this kind of process is the loss in English of non-prevocalic /r/ in words like *cart* and *car*, which we discussed in Chapter 1. Map 1 is based on the survey of conservative rural dialects carried out under the direction of Harold Orton at the University of Leeds, and shows those areas of England where loss of non-prevocalic /r/ in the pronunciation of the words *farm* or *yard* has not yet taken place. If we did not know already from other sources (such as the spelling) that it is the form without /r/ which is the newer, the separation of the three relatively peripheral areas shown on the map (the south-west, the north-west, and the north-east, spreading up into Scotland) would suggest most strongly that this was the case. (An identical innovation is unlikely to start in three separate areas at once.) The configuration of r-pronouncing areas on the map also suggests that the innovation began somewhere in the centre or east of England before spreading north and west, although we cannot be certain, from the map alone, *when* the innovation began.

Sociolinguistically speaking, this map represents a considerable simplification of the true state of affairs concerning non-prevocalic /r/ in England. First, it is confined to only two words: an examination of data for other words would reveal additional areas, such as parts of east Yorkshire, where non-prevocalic /r/ may be pronounced. Secondly, it is socially very incomplete. All along the eastern edge of the south-western area, for instance, it is only older speakers from the lowest social groups who are 'r-pronouncers', and even they are likely to use an /r/ less frequently and pronounce it less strongly than speakers further south and west. Thirdly, the map gives information only for rural linguistic varieties. For many urban areas, particularly the larger towns, the impression given is very inaccurate since, unlike the rural areas, they may be entirely 'r-less' (this is true of Liverpool, for example).

The reason for this difference between urban and rural

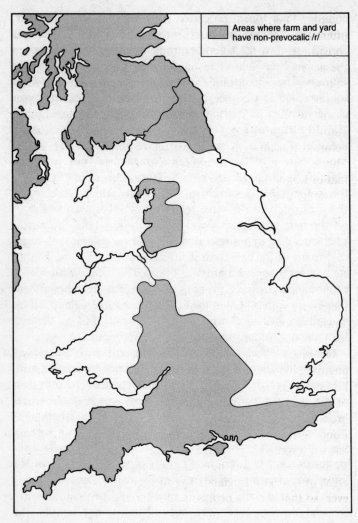

Areas where farm and yard
have non-prevocalic /r/

Map 1. Non-prevocalic /r/ in yard *and* farm *in conservative rural dialects in England*

accents is that linguistic innovations, like other innovations, often spread from one urban centre to another, and only later spread out into the surrounding countryside. This is due to the general economic, demographic and cultural dominance of town over country, and to the structure of the communication network. The spread of linguistic features from one area to another is therefore not dependent solely on proximity. An innovation starting in London is quite likely to reach Bristol before it reaches rural Wiltshire, although the latter is nearer. The speech of Manchester, too, is in many ways more like that of London than of nearby rural Cheshire:

	London	Manchester	Hyde, Cheshire
'brush'	[brʌš]	[broš]	[brəiš]
'such'	[sʌč]	[soč]	[sɪč]
'tough'	[tʌf]	[tʊf]	[tɒf]
'put'	[pʊt]	[pʊt]	[pʊr]

The Manchester and London forms are not identical, but there is a regular relationship such that all London [ʌ] and [ʊ] vowels correspond to Manchester [ʊ] vowels. In the case of the Hyde forms there is no such regular correspondence.

One interesting problem for sociolinguistics is why some linguistic innovations spread faster than others. The difference between London [ʌ] and Manchester [ʊ] in *tough* is the result of the original pronunciation [ʊ] being replaced by a new pronunciation [ʌ], which started life as an innovation in London, probably in the sixteenth century. This innovation has since spread northwards and westwards, but has travelled so slowly that it has not yet reached Manchester or other areas of northern England. The merger of /f/ and /θ/, however, so that *thing* is pronounced *fing*, was for many decades a well-known feature of London English only. Suddenly, though, in recent years, it has started spreading very rapidly outwards from London. It seems to have arrived in Norwich in the 1970s, in Sheffield in the north of England in the 1980s, and in Exeter in the south-west in the 1990s.

Distance, then, is clearly an important factor in the spread of linguistic forms, although in many cases social distance may be as important as geographical distance, as we have just seen: two towns may be socially 'closer' to each other than they are to the intervening stretches of countryside. What of barriers? We mentioned, in Chapter 2, the role of social barriers in the formation of social-class dialects, and the way in which the River Humber had acted as a geographical barrier to the spread of linguistic features in the north of England. There is also a third type of barrier which surprisingly enough does not necessarily have a significant slowing-down effect – namely the *language barrier*. Linguistic innovations, it appears, spread not only from one regional or social variety of the same language to another; they *may* also spread from one language into another.

An interesting example of a linguistic feature that has spread in this way is the European *uvular r*. It is thought that up until at least the sixteenth century all European languages had an r-type sound which was pronounced as r still is pronounced today in many types of Scots English or Italian: a tongue-tip trill (roll) or flap. At some stage, though, perhaps in the seventeenth century, a new pronunciation of r became fashionable in upper-class Parisian French. This new r, uvular r [R], is pronounced in the back of the mouth by means of contact between the back of the tongue and the uvula – technically a uvular trill, flap, fricative or frictionless continuant sound – and is the type of r sound taught today to foreign learners of French and German. Starting from this limited social and geographical base, the uvular-r pronunciation has during the last 300 years spread, regardless of language boundaries, to many other parts of Europe, as Map 2 shows. It is now used by the overwhelming majority of urban or educated French speakers, and by most educated Germans. Some Dutch speakers use it, as do nearly all Danes, together with a majority in the south of Sweden and parts of the south and west of Norway. On the other hand, it is not used in Bavarian or, for the most part, Swiss German, nor, except by a small minority, in Italian. (The uvular r is also a feature of local English accents in parts of Northumberland and Durham. It is not clear whether this phenomenon is connected to the continental pronunciation or not.)

Processes of this type generally, when they involve grammar and vocabulary as well as phonetics and phonology, can lead to the development of *linguistic areas*. This term is used to refer to areas where several languages are spoken which, although they are not necessarily very closely related, have a number of features in common, as a result of the diffusion of innovations across language boundaries. One of the most interesting areas of this kind in Europe is the Balkans, comprising former Yugoslavia, Albania, Greece, Bulgaria and Romania. The languages involved are Serbo-Croat, Macedonian and Bulgarian (all Slav languages), Rumanian (a Romance language), Greek, and Albanian. These are all Indo-European languages, but apart from the three Slav languages they are not closely related genetically. Over the centuries, they have acquired a number of common features sometimes known as 'Balkanisms' which mark some or all of them off from other (often more closely related) European languages. Rumanian and Bulgarian, for example, have a number of common features which are not shared by any other Romance or Slav languages.

One of the most interesting features of the Balkan languages is the fact that four of them have a postposed definite article: the form corresponding to *the* in English is placed after the noun:

Albanian:	mekanik*u*
Bulgarian:	mexanik*ut*
Macedonian:	mexaničar*ot*
Rumanian:	mecanician*ul*
	'*the* mechanic'

(The only other European languages to have this feature are the Scandinavian languages.) Another grammatical feature shared by many of the Balkan languages is a particular usage of subordinate clauses. Most European languages employ a construction where English has:

They left without asking me

which corresponds in English to:

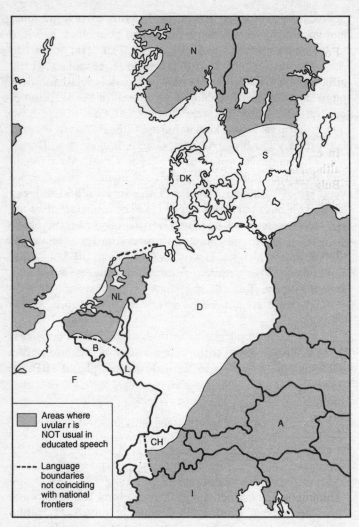

Map 2. Uvular r in Europe

'They left without to ask me.'

For example:

> 'They left . . .'
>> French: . . . *sans me* demander
>> German: . . . *ohne mich* zu fragen
>> Danish: . . . *uden* at spørge *mig.*

In each case a construction with an infinitive can be used, although other constructions may be possible. In Albanian, Bulgarian, Greek, and Rumanian, on the other hand, another construction is usual, equivalent in English to:

> 'They left without that they asked me.'

For example:

> 'They left . . .'
>> Bulgarian: . . . *bez da me popitat*
>> Greek: . . . *xoris na me rotisune*
>> '. . . without that me they asked.'

Many other examples of linguistic areas can be found in different parts of the world. The Indian subcontinent is a good instance of an area where non-related languages have a number of features in common. Generally speaking, the majority of north Indian languages belong to the Indo-European family, while most of the languages spoken in the south of India are Dravidian. As far as we know, these language groups are not related at all. However, in spite of this lack of relationship, many Indian languages from both groups have grammatical constructions in common, and share a number of features of pronunciation. One of the most striking phonetic similarities is the presence in both families of retroflex consonants: consonants formed by curling the tip of the tongue back and bringing it into contact with the back of the alveolar ridge. (Consonant articulations of this type are a noticeable feature of the English pronunciation of speakers from the Indian subcontinent.) For example:

Dravidian languages	Tamil:	/koḍai/	'umbrella'
	Coorg:	/kaḍi/	'bite'
Indo-European languages	Marathi:	/ghoḍa/	'horse'
	Hindi:	/gaːḍi/	'cart'

Another comparable example is provided by certain of the languages of southern Africa, comprising several Khoisan (Bushman and Hottentot) languages, which are probably all related to each other, and a number of Bantu languages (which are definitely not related to Khoisan) including Sotho, Zulu and Xhosa. These languages have a number of phonetic features in common, notably the presence of 'clicks' as consonants. ('Clicks' include sounds like that represented in English orthography as *tut-tut*, as well as the clicking noise made, in Britain at least, to encourage horses.) The letter *x* in Xhosa, incidentally, represents one particular type of click sound.

Linguistic innovations, then, can spread from one dialect into another adjacent dialect. If spreading of this type takes place across language boundaries, on a sufficiently large scale, linguistic areas are formed. Broadly speaking, though, it appears that only grammatical and phonological features require geographical proximity before diffusion of this sort can take place. (Uvular r can now be found in Norway, but it almost certainly arrived there from France via Germany and Denmark.) Lexical items appear to be able to spread across much greater distances. Words can be borrowed from one language into another regardless of proximity. Very often, when speakers of a particular language happen to be dominant in some particular field, other language groups adopt words pertaining to the field from this language. For example, many English musical terms – like *adagio, allegro, crescendo* – are of Italian origin, while sporting terms in many languages, like *football, goal, sprint*, as well as terms connected with pop music and jazz, tend to be English. At present, English is a source of loan words for very many languages, particularly in Europe. Borrowings of this type take place initially through the medium of the bilingual individual (there must be somebody who knows the foreign word in the first place), and individuals bilingual in English along with their native language are becoming increasingly common as the result of the widespread use of English as a lingua franca and its correspondingly widespread teaching in schools. This, of course, is not due to any inherent superiority of the English language as a medium of international communication, but rather to the former world political, economic, educational and scientific dominance of Britain and the similar present dominance of the USA.

The use of English as a lingua franca brings us to a rather different aspect of the geographical spread of linguistic phenomena. So far, we have confined our attention to those cases where features of a language can spread from person to person, group to group, and eventually, by this means – as in the case of uvular r – 'travel' over very large distances. Another equally important method by means of which linguistic forms may spread is for the speakers themselves to travel. (Uvular r might have arrived in Norway much sooner if large numbers of Parisians had emigrated to Norway, or had had extensive trade contacts there.) When, as the result of travel, speakers of different languages come into contact with each other, they may have to communicate by means of a lingua franca (see p. 133).

Now, when English is used as a lingua franca in Europe, as it often is if, say, a Dutchman and a Swede want to talk to one another, it is frequently spoken with a great deal of fluency and expertise, usually as a result of many years' formal tuition in schools. Even so, it is still rather unusual to find a non-native speaker who uses English as a lingua franca who can speak English as well, and use it in as many different social situations, as a native English speaker. In other words, when a language is used as a lingua franca it normally undergoes a certain amount of simplification and reduction – as well as being subject to the introduction of errors through interference from the native language of the speaker.

Simplification is, paradoxically, a rather complex notion,

but it refers most often to getting rid of irregularities, such as irregular verb forms, and redundancies, such as grammatical gender, in the lingua franca. This normally happens because, unlike small children, adults are generally not particularly good language learners. Reduction refers to the fact that, as a result of a reduction in social function, lingua franca speakers may use the language for doing business, but not perhaps for playing football or doing the washing-up, and means that, compared to the usage of a native speaker, parts of the language are missing: vocabulary, grammatical structures, stylistic devices. The technical term for the process by which languages may be subject, in the usage of non-native speakers, to simplification, reduction and interference is *pidginization*. Pidginization may be slight (as perhaps in the case of educated Dutch and Swedish speakers). On the other hand, where little or no formal schooling has taken place, it may be much larger; and where learning takes place only through intermittent and limited contacts, it may be very great indeed. This point can be illustrated from the case of Swahili, which, as we have seen, is widely used as a lingua franca in East Africa. On parts of the coast of East Africa, Swahili is the native language of many of the population, who use it for all or most purposes and, naturally enough, speak it very fluently. Inland in Tanzania it is not widely spoken natively, but it is used to a considerable extent as a lingua franca. Compared to the coastal Swahili this inland lingua-franca variety demonstrates some features of simplification, since it is spoken as a second language, and it is subject to reduction, for it is used in a more restricted set of circumstances than on the coast. Further inland still, in eastern Zaïre, yet another variety of Swahili is used as a lingua franca. In this case, even more reduction and simplification have taken place. Simplification here refers to the absence of irregular verbs, the reduction in the number of noun classes (genders), and the avoidance of certain complex syntactic structures. Both these lingua-franca varieties of Swahili, although modified, are clearly nevertheless to be counted as Swahili. They are intelligible to coastal Swahili speakers, apparently, and native speakers of Swahili do not have to make very many concessions when talking to lingua-franca users in order to make themselves understood.

However, in another part of Zaïre, in the rural north, a further lingua-franca form of Swahili occurs. This variety again is reduced and simplified, relative to coastal Swahili, but much more so. Verb structures, for example, are radically simplified, there are no noun classes, and only a relatively limited number of sentence structures is employed. The result of this degree of reduction and simplification, it is said, is that mutual intelligibility with coastal Swahili is minimal. The language is used only as a lingua franca, yet if native Swahili speakers want to employ it as such they have to *learn* it – at least to a certain extent. When pidginization has taken place on this scale, and when the result is a relatively stabilized form of language consistently employed as a lingua franca, the resulting variety is called a *pidgin* language (in this case we call it Zaïre Pidgin Swahili).

A pidgin language, then, is a lingua franca which has no native speakers. Chronologically speaking, it is derived from a 'normal' language through simplification, reduction and interference or admixture, often considerable, from the native language or languages of those who use it, especially so far as pronunciation is concerned. Normally, in the first stages of its development at least, in which we can refer to it as a *pre-pidgin*, it is used only in trading or other limited-contact situations. (Where contacts are more permanent, fuller second-language learning is more likely to result.)

The most likely setting for the crystallization of a true pidgin language is probably a contact situation of this limited type involving three or more language groups: one 'dominant' language (in the case we have just discussed, Swahili), and at least two 'non-dominant' languages. If contact between the speakers of the dominant language and the others is minimal, and the imperfectly learned dominant language is then used as a lingua franca among the non-dominant groups, it is not difficult to see how a pidgin might arise. Over time, in the speech of lingua franca users, the pre-pidgin will acquire a set of structures and norms for usage which will be accepted by everybody. It will acquire, as a result of what sociolinguists call *focusing*, a fixed form which linguists can describe and write grammars of. The resulting *pidgin* thus differs from *pidginized* forms of language, which vary from time to time and from speaker to speaker. (The same sort of development might well take place if a Swedish schoolchild and a Dutch schoolchild, each with one year's study of English, were marooned alone on a desert island: they would probably develop, out of their individual, pidginized form of English, a Dutch–Swedish Pidgin English as their mode of communication.) Moreover, it is possible that certain universal processes of simplification may play a part in the formation of pidgins. We shall discuss this last point briefly below.

It is important to realize that pidgins, although rather different from other languages, are really different in degree rather than in kind. They are genuine languages with structure and most of the attributes of other languages. They are difficult to learn properly, although probably easier than other languages (particularly for speakers of the languages dominant in their formation). Pidgins are not, therefore – as has often been maintained – haphazard mixtures, nor are they 'bad', 'debased' or 'corrupt' forms of the language from which they are derived. Consider the following example of British Solomon Islands Pidgin, often known as Neo-Solomonic by linguists, which is widely used as a lingua franca in the Solomon Islands:

Mifɛlə i-go go lɔŋ sɔlwater, lʊkautım fıš, nau wm i-kəm. Nau mifɛlə i-go ɔləbaut lɔŋ kinú, nau bıgfɛlə wın i-kəm nau, mifɛlə i-fafasi ɔləbautə, rɔŋ tuməs.

'We kept going on the sea, hunting for fish, and a wind arose. Now we were going in canoes, and an immense wind arose now, and we were thrown around and were moving very fast.'

Clearly, if one regards this as a form of English, then it is a very strange kind of English indeed. It is difficult to understand for an English speaker, particularly when heard rather than read, and the translation is necessary, I think. Similarly, if it is regarded as the result of an attempt by the speaker to learn English as a foreign language, then it is a very unsuccessful attempt. However, strictly speaking it is neither of those things. The speaker here *has* learnt a second language, but the second language he learnt was Neo-Solomonic, not English. The grammar and vocabulary of Neo-Solomonic, although similar to English in many ways, is nonetheless quite distinct. The language has grammatical rules and words of its own. For example, *kaikai*, Neo-Solomonic for 'food, eat', is not an English word; and the requirement that transitive verbs be distinguished from intransitives (by the suffix *-im* – compare *lokautim* with *go*) is not a grammatical rule of English. It is therefore quite desirable, on linguistic grounds alone, to regard Neo-Solomonic, and other varieties of Pidgin English, as languages quite separate from English (although obviously related to it). Another good, social, reason for doing this is that many people have objected to pidgins on the grounds that they have corrupted the 'purity' of English (or some other European language). Views like this are often accompanied by sentiments about racial and cultural 'purity' as well. If one regards a pidgin as a debased and inferior form of English, it may be quite easy to regard its speakers, mostly non-Europeans, as also being 'debased' and 'inferior'. One point that a linguist can make when faced with views such as these is to point out that there is no such thing as a 'pure' language. All languages are subject to change, and they are all the product of influence and admixture from other languages. (Take vocabulary alone: of the fifteen different words in my previous sentence, seven have been borrowed by English from foreign languages during the past 1,000 years.)

Most of the better-known pidgin languages in the world are the result of travel on the part of European traders and colonizers. They are based on languages like English, French and Portuguese, and are located on the main shipping and trading routes. English-based pidgins were formerly found in North America, at both ends of the slave trade in Africa and the Caribbean, in New Zealand and in China. They are still found in Australia, West Africa, the Solomon Islands (as we have seen) and in New Guinea, where Pidgin English is often referred to by linguists as Tok Pisin, the name for the language *in* the language. Not all pidgin languages have arisen in this way, though. Kituba, which is derived from Kikongo, a Bantu language, is a pidgin widely used in western Zaïre and adjoining areas. And Fanagolo, which is based on Zulu, is a pidgin spoken in South Africa and adjoining countries, particularly in the mines. There are several other indigenous pidgins in Africa and elsewhere.

Tok Pisin is probably the most widely spoken pidgin derived from English. It has official status in Papua New Guinea, and is used there on the radio, in newspapers, and in schools. At present, in fact, it is undergoing quite considerable *creolization*. As we saw in Chapter 3, creole languages are pidgins that have acquired native speakers. In linguistically mixed communities where a pidgin is used as the lingua franca, children may acquire it as their native language, particularly if their parents normally communicate in the pidgin. When this occurs the language will re-acquire all the characteristics of a full, non-pidgin language. As spoken by an adult native speaker the language will have, when compared to the original pidgin, an expanded vocabulary, a wider range of syntactic possibilities, and an increased stylistic repertoire. It will also, of course, be used for all purposes in a full range of social situations. That is, the reduction that occurred during pidginization will be repaired, although the simplification and admixture will remain. (Notice that *simplification* is a technical, not a value-loaded, term. Creole languages are not in some intellectual sense simpler than their source languages. They are, rather, more regular and less redundant.) This process whereby reduction is 'repaired' by expansion is known as *creolization* and is one of the most fascinating processes of all in linguistic change. Derek Bickerton has argued that children, needing to use a pidgin language as their native language, expand it in part by calling on the genetic mental resources all human beings are born with – the human language faculty – and that creolization thus provides us with an unusual and fascinating window into the human mind. Creole languages, in other words, are perfectly normal languages – only their history is somewhat unusual.

Of European-based creole languages – those that have developed out of pidgins based on European languages – the best known are French, English, Portuguese and Spanish creoles. French creoles are widely spoken in the Caribbean and adjoining areas: Haiti, where Haitian French Creole is the native language of the vast majority of the population; Trinidad and Grenada, and other islands in the southern Caribbean; French Guiana; and the United States, where a French creole is spoken by Blacks in parts of Louisiana. French creoles are also spoken in the Indian Ocean, notably in Mauritius and the Seychelles. The following extract from the Lord's Prayer in Haitian Creole indicates the extent of the relationship between this creole and French:

Papa nou, ki nan sièl, ké non ou jouinn tout réspè. Ké règn ou vini. Ké volonté ou akonpli sou tè a tankou nan sièl. Ban nou, jodi a, pin chak jou nou.

Most of the better-known English creoles are spoken in different parts of the Americas and, like the French creoles, are a consequence of the slave trade. Sranan, for example, is an English creole spoken by several tens of thousands of native speakers in coastal areas of Surinam, and is also widely used by others in the area as a lingua franca. Here is an example (see also p. 59):

Ala den bigibigi man de na balkon e wakti en. A kon nanga en buku na ondro en anu. A puru en ati na en ede, en a meki kosi gi den. Dan a waka go na a djari, pe den gansi de.

'All the important men were on the balcony waiting for him. He came with his book under his arm. He took off his hat and bowed before them. Then he went to the garden where the geese were.'

Sranan is one of the most 'conservative' of English creoles, i.e. it has been very little affected by influence from English, and it gives us a good idea of what other less isolated creoles may have been like at earlier stages of their history.

Inland in Surinam other English creoles are spoken, mainly

by the descendants of runaway slaves who succeeded in fleeing into the jungle. The best known of these creoles – which are apparently not intelligible to Sranan speakers – is Djuka. Just to make things more complicated, Djuka is apparently also spoken in pidginized form as a lingua franca by groups of Amerindians living in the area. This last variety has therefore had a history something like this:

$$
\begin{array}{ll}
\text{English} & \\
\quad\downarrow & \text{(pidginization)} \\
\text{West African Pidgin} & \\
\quad\downarrow & \text{(creolization)} \\
\text{Djuka} & \\
\quad\downarrow & \text{(pidginization)} \\
\text{Pidgin Djuka} &
\end{array}
$$

Both Sranan and Djuka are uncontroversial, socially and linguistically. They are recognized by all to be creoles, and as languages distinct from English: it would be difficult to make out a good case for the above specimen of Sranan as a type of English. Mutual intelligibility between Sranan and English is nil. Socially, too, there are no reasons for regarding Sranan as a form of English. Dutch is the official language in Surinam, and English itself is little used. In other parts of the world, however, the position is much less clear. In parts of West Africa, for instance, Pidgin English is widely employed as a lingua franca, and in certain areas, notably in parts of Nigeria, it has become creolized. The difficulty there is that, in contrast to Surinam, English is an official language and is used, as a 'world language' of high prestige, in many different functions throughout the country. The result of this is that Nigerian Pidgin, even in its creolized form, has become heteronomous (see p. 4) with respect to Standard British and/or Nigerian English. Pidgin English is subject to considerable influence from English, and is widely considered simply to be a 'bad' or 'corrupt' form of English.

In Sierra Leone the situation is similar, although if anything rather more complicated. In Freetown, the capital, it is possible, probably somewhat artificially, to distinguish between four different linguistic varieties which have some connection with English:

1. British English;
2. Sierra Leone English – spoken mainly by middle-
   class Sierra Leonians, and containing certain
   features due to the influence of African languages;
3. West African Pidgin English – used as a (mainly
   commercial) lingua franca;
4. Krio.

Krio is an English creole with about 30,000 native speakers living in and around Freetown. The language developed from an English creole spoken by slaves returned from Jamaica, North America and Britain, and is not directly connected with West African Pidgin. The following four versions of the same sentence illustrate some of the similarities and differences involved:

British English:	/aɪm goʊɪŋ tə wɜːk/
Sierra Leone English:	/aim goin to wɔk/
West African Pidgin:	/a di go wɔk/
Krio:	/a de go wok/

The similarities between the four varieties inevitably lead to the conclusion on the part of most Sierra Leonians that the three lower prestige forms represent unsuccessful attempts to imitate the higher prestige British English – and Pidgin and Krio in particular are often simply regarded as 'broken English'.

In parts of the formerly British West Indies the position is again similar, but the problems it brings with it are considerably more severe. Let us consider Jamaica. Some linguists writing about the language spoken in Jamaica refer to it as *Jamaican English* while others, preferring to give it the status of a separate language, call it *Jamaican Creole*. This disagreement about terminology is the result of the discreteness and continuity problem we mentioned in Chapter 1 (p. 4). In Jamaica, Standard English is the official language and is spoken there, at the top of the social scale, by educated

Jamaicans and some people of British origin. At the other end of the social scale, particularly in the case of peasants in isolated rural areas, the language used is an English-based creole which is not in itself mutually intelligible with Standard (or any other form of) English. The linguistic differences are great enough for us to be able to say, if these two varieties were the only two involved, that, like Sranan, Jamaican Creole is a language related to but distinct from English. To help make this point, here is an extract from a creole text cited by a Jamaican-Creole scholar, Beryl Bailey:

Wantaim, wan man en ha wan gyal-pikni nomo. Im ena wan priti gyal fi-truu. Im neba laik fi taak tu eni an eni man. Im laik a nais buosi man fi taak tu. Im taat taak tu wan man, bot im get kalops aafta im taak tu di man.

'Once upon a time, there was a gentleman who had an only daughter. She was a gay and dandy girl. She didn't like to talk to just any man. She wanted a gay, fine man to talk to. She started to talk to a man, but she got pregnant by talking to the man.' (Beryl Bailey's translation is into Jamaican rather than British Standard English.)

The problem is, however, that between these two extremes, at intermediate points on the social scale, there is a whole range of intermediate varieties which connect the two in a chain of mutual intelligibility. There is, in other words, a social-dialect continuum ranging from Standard English to 'deepest' Jamaican Creole. This means that all language varieties in Jamaica have become heteronomous·with respect to Standard English, even if they are not really mutually comprehensible with it. In fact the social-dialect continuum itself may well have arisen in the first place as a result of the influence of high-prestige English on low-status Creole: the stronger the influence, the more *decreolization* would take place. And the influence of English shows no sign of diminishing. Certainly, even 'deepest' Creole, as our text shows, is much more like English than Sranan is. Unlike creolization, which 'repairs' the reduction which takes place during pidginization, *decreolization* is a process which attacks the simplification and admixture which occur during pidginization. Contact between the source language (in this case English) and a creole language such as Jamaican Creole leads to the gradual introduction into the Creole of irregularities and redundancies from the source language, and the gradual disappearance of elements derived from languages other than the source – such as, in this case, words derived from African languages.

The problems caused by the English–Creole continuum in Jamaica, often referred to as a *post-creole continuum*, are quite considerable. In Chapter 1, when we were talking about geographical dialect continua, we saw that, in the case of Dutch and German dialects, it was possible to make a (linguistically arbitrary) decision as to which varieties were dialects of which language, simply by using the political frontier. In Jamaica no equivalent 'social frontier' exists: we cannot place a clear dividing line between Creole and English. But if, as a consequence, we consider, as most people do, that the language of all Jamaicans is 'English', a number of problems may arise.

First, there is a very widespread view in Jamaica (as elsewhere in the Caribbean) that the majority of Jamaicans speak a very inferior type of English (since Jamaican Creole is obviously so different from English). Secondly, it means that children are taught to read and write in Standard English; after all, 'English' is considered to be their language. Because of the great differences between English and many types of creole, however, many of these children never succeed in learning to read or write English with any degree of proficiency, and the failure rate of Jamaican children taking British English examinations is very high, compared to their performance in other subjects.

From a purely linguistic point of view, a sensible solution to this state of affairs would be a Norwegian type of approach (forgetting for the moment that there are two Standard Norwegians). In spite of the fact that Standard Danish was similar to Norwegian dialects, to the extent that they were formerly felt to be heteronomous with respect to Danish, Norway developed its own standard language after political independence had been achieved. This new standard language was still similar to Danish, but was sufficiently different from it to make it resemble actual Norwegian speech much more closely. In Jamaica, and elsewhere, it would be possible to do the same sort of thing. A new Standard Jamaican Creole (or English) could be developed that would reflect much more closely the nature of the language spoken by Jamaicans. It would resemble English, but would nevertheless be regarded as a different language. English could then be learnt later, once literacy had been acquired, as a semi-foreign language, much as Norwegians now learn to read and understand Danish and Swedish.

In practice, however, there are a great number of obstacles to a solution of this type. English is a statusful language which is also very useful as a lingua franca, and it is the language of a culture which is powerful and influential in Jamaica. The political and social relationship between Jamaican Creole and English is therefore not exactly the same as that which existed between Danish and Norwegian. Few nineteenth-century Norwegians would have been upset by statements to the effect that they did not speak Danish. On the other hand, many West Indians might feel insulted by suggestions that they do not speak English. This is because (a) varieties near the (social) top of the Jamaican dialect continuum are much more like English than Creole – there is no real linguistic reason for saying they are 'not English', and (b) it is a characteristic of social attitudes to language that they tend to be shared even by those who suffer most from those attitudes: Standard English is accepted by nearly everybody in Jamaica as 'good' and deviations from it as 'bad'. Further, because of the prestige of Standard English, those who have already mastered it would not readily relinquish the social and financial advantages it has brought them. People would be conscious, too, of the danger of becoming isolated from the rest of the English-speaking world. The main problem, though, would be one of people's social attitudes about the appropriateness of certain linguistic varieties to certain social contexts. To read the BBC news in a 'broad'

London, Birmingham or Glasgow accent would provoke laughter, anger, and ridicule. The same kind of reaction could be expected to the introduction of Jamaican Creole into unexpected contexts. It could be done, however, if a political decision were made to do so: English would have sounded ridiculous in a law-court in the Middle Ages, and would have been considered out of place in a scientific treatise at a much later date than that; a piece of literature in Finnish would have been considered most unusual until comparatively recently; and the use of Macedonian as a parliamentary language would have been felt to be absurd until this century.

From a more theoretical linguistic point of view, one of the most interesting features of creole languages generally – at least in the case of those related historically to European languages – is the number of similarities they share with one another, regardless of geographical location. Consider the following verb forms:

Jamaican Creole:	/wa de go hapm nou/	'What's going to happen now?'
Sranan:	/mi de kom/	'I'm coming.'
Gullah:	/de də njam forə/	'They were eating fodder.'
Krio:	/a de go wok/	'I'm going to work.'

(Jamaican Creole is, geographically, Caribbean; Sranan, South American; Gullah [see also p. 59], North American; and Krio, West African.) The above sentences all demonstrate what can be called *progressive* or *continuous aspect*: they concern not single short-lived actions, but actions taking place over a relatively longer period of time. (This is revealed in the English translations by verb forms with *be* + verb-*ing*.) The similarities to note are as follows:

1. All these creoles are able to mark continuous aspect without marking tense. (The Gullah example has been translated as past, but in other contexts it could equally well be present.)

2. All the creoles show continuous aspect, not by an inflec-

tion of the verb, as in English, but by a particle – an independent word standing before the verb.

3. The actual form of this particle is almost identical in each case: *de, de, də, de*.

These similarities are even more striking if we note that French-based creoles demonstrate exactly the same verb structure:

pronoun + continuous-aspect particle + verb

Louisiana FC:	/mo ape travaj/	'I am working.'
Haitian FC:	/yo ape mãze/	'They are eating.'
Mauritius FC:	/ki to ape fer/	'What are you doing?'

Note, too, that once again the form of the particle is identical /ape/ (historically related to French *après*), in spite of the several thousand miles which separate Mauritius from the Caribbean. Portuguese creoles, too, have the same construction:

pronoun + particle + verb

St Thomas Portuguese Creole: /e ka nda/ 'He is going.'

How can we explain the similarities (both of structure and of form) between these languages, particularly in view of the great distances separating them and of the fact that they appear to be historically derived from different sources? One explanation that has been put forward stresses the similarity of those situations which led to the growth of pidgins (and hence of creoles). These languages were generally the joint creation of sailors, traders and indigenous peoples in trading or other similar contexts, it is pointed out, and it is therefore not surprising that these languages are similar. It is also true that pidgins grow up in circumstances where the transmission of information is very difficult and where it may be very useful to make language as simple and efficient an instrument of communication as possible. That is, there may be universal or widespread principles of simplification – including the loss of redundant features and the omission of irregularities – which will favour some structures more than others.

A second explanation goes under the name of the 'relexification theory'. Briefly, this theory claims that the first widespread European-based pidgin was Portuguese Pidgin, which probably grew up some time during the fifteenth century along the West African coast. The Portuguese then spread it to their other trading posts and colonies in Africa and Asia, and traders from other countries began to learn it as well. However, when French and English traders entered the trade – particularly the slave trade – in large numbers, *relexification* of this Portuguese pidgin took place. The grammar of the language remained the same, but the *words* were changed. Words derived from Portuguese were gradually replaced by words from English, French, or some other dominant European language. The evidence in favour of this theory is as follows:

1. Some Portuguese words still remain in many non-Portuguese pidgins and creoles e.g. *savvy*, from Portuguese *sabe*, 'he knows', and *piccaninny*, from Portuguese *pequenino*, 'little'.

2. A large number of words found in creole languages can be traced back to West African languages. For example, /njam/ 'eat', which is found in Jamaican Creole, Gullah, Sranan, and others, probably derives from /njami/, which means 'to eat' in Fulani, a language spoken today in Guinea, Gambia, Senegal and Mali.

3. There are a number of grammatical similarities, in addition to those we have already noted in the case of verbs, between English, French, Portuguese and other creoles. The 'same grammar but different words' hypothesis provides a ready explanation for this.

4. The actual nature of the grammatical similarities – although they may be partly due to universal principles of simplification – suggests links with West African languages. Many of these languages, like the creoles, indicate aspect and tense by means of preposed particles, for instance. Compare:

Louisiana French Creole:	/mo to kupe/	'I (past) cut.'
St Thomas Portuguese Creole:	/e ta nda/	'He (past) go.'
Yoruba:	/mo ti wa/	'I (past) come.'

One final piece of evidence for the relexification hypothesis may be provided by Saramakkan. This is a creole language also spoken in Surinam. It appears that this creole may have been arrested, by the flight of the slaves who spoke it into the jungle, at a half-way stage of transfer from Portuguese- to English-derived vocabulary. It is most often considered to be a Portuguese creole, but the English element in the vocabulary is very large.

A third explanation relates to the work of Derek Bickerton, mentioned above. If all creoles are the result of expansion, by children, of a pidgin language; and if the children of these different communities all had to draw on their innate knowledge of what human language in general – as opposed to any language in particular – is like in order to do this; and if the human language faculty is something which all human beings share – which is undoubtedly the case; then it is perhaps not surprising that creoles around the world have similar structures.

As we saw in Chapter 3, many linguists have argued that AAVE is descended from an original creole that has become progressively decreolized, as a result of centuries of contact with English, so that it is now clearly a variety of English itself. If this is correct, we can say, just as we used the term *post-creole* to refer to the situation in Jamaica, that AAVE is a *late* or *vestigial post-creole*. Recall that decreolization attacks the simplification and admixture that took place during pidginization. If we call the reverse of simplification *complication* and the reverse of admixture *purification* (notice that this is a technical term without any value-loading – *purification* does not make a language more or less desirable in any way), then this gives us the following chronological picture:

Process:	pidginization	focusing	creolization	partial decreolization	further decreolization
Source →	Pre-pidgin →	Pidgin →	Creole →	Post-creole →	Vestigial Post-creole
	simplification admixture reduction		expansion	complication purification	complication purification

Of course, if the processes of complication and purification were eventually to be total, then a *vestigial post-creole* like AAVE would end up having no creole features at all, giving no clues to its creole history.

Interestingly, there are some languages in the world which look like post-creoles, but which are not. These are varieties which, compared to some source, show a certain degree of simplification and admixture. We do not, however, call these languages creoles, because the extent of the simplification and admixture is not very great. And we do not call them post-creoles because they have never been creoles – which is in turn because they have never been pidgins! Afrikaans, the other major language of the white community in South Africa alongside English, used to be considered a dialect of Dutch, as we saw earlier. During the course of this century, however, it has achieved autonomy (see Chapter 1) and now has its own literature, dictionaries, grammar books, and so on. Compared to Dutch, Afrikaans shows significant amounts of regularization in the grammar, and a significant amount of admixture from Malay, Portuguese and other languages. It still remains mutually intelligible with Dutch, however. The crucial feature of Afrikaans is that, although it is now spoken by some South Africans who are the descendants of people who spoke it as a non-native language – hence the influence from Portuguese, Malay, and so on – and who undoubtedly therefore spoke a *pidginized* form of Dutch/Afrikaans, the language was at no time a pidgin. In the transition from Dutch to Afrikaans, the native-speaker tradition was maintained throughout. The language was passed down from one generation of native speakers to another; it was used for all social functions and was therefore never subjected to reduction. Such a language, which demonstrates a certain amount of *simplification* and *admixture*, relative to some source language, but which has never been a pidgin or a creole in the sense that it has always had speakers who spoke a variety which was not subject to reduction, we can call a *creoloid*.

Pidgins, creoles and creoloids are all languages that result from contact between languages and are therefore 'mixed' languages. All the pidgins, creoles and creoloids we have discussed so far, however, have had a single main source. It is clear, for example, that Neo-Solomonic is an *English*-based pidgin, that Haitian Creole is a *French*-based creole, that Jamaican English is an *English*-based post-creole, and that Afrikaans is a *Dutch*-based creoloid.

There are other fascinating cases around the world, however, where languages of this type appear to have two main sources. We can call these languages *dual-source* pidgins, creoles, post-creoles and creoloids. Russenorsk was a pidgin spoken in the far north of Norway until 1917, when trade between Norway and Russia halted as a result of the Russian revolution. It was a reduced and simplified language which consisted of elements taken from Russian and Norwegian in about equal measure. It obviously arose as a result of contact between Russian and Norwegian speakers, but it acquired focused norms of usage, and was also learnt and used as a lingua franca by speakers of other languages such as Sami, Finnish, Dutch, German and English. It is probably significant that Russenorsk arose not in a colonial situation but in a European trading setting in which both contributing languages were spoken by people of approximately equivalent wealth and technology.

It is difficult to imagine situations in which such dual-source pidgins could become the sole language of a community, and hence give rise to creoles. At least one such situation has occurred, however. Pitcairnese, the language of the remote Pacific Ocean island Pitcairn, is a dual-source creole which is the sole native language of the small community there. The Pitcairnese are for the most part descendants of the British sailors who carried out the famous mutiny on the *Bounty* and Tahitian men and women who went with them to hide on Pitcairn from the British Royal Navy. Their language is a mixed and simplified form of English and Tahitian (a Polynesian language), as can be seen below:

got a pur^{2}iti fə puš em ho^2 ston – wen em bin put in a weku, hem jʌmu fə plente lif ən pehu plente dɔ:^{2}

'There was a stick for pushing those hot stones. When they had put in the food, they wrapped it in a lot of leaves and covered it with a lot of earth.'

Pitcairnese also has speakers on Norfolk Island, in the Western Pacific, who are descended from people who resettled there from Pitcairn. On Norfolk Island, the language is in close contact with Australian English, and is consequently decreolizing (in the direction of English, not Tahitian). We can therefore describe it as a dual-source post-creole.

There are also languages that one can refer to as dual-source creoloids. One such language is Michif (Metsif, Métis – there are various spellings), which has its origins in Canada but most of whose 'mixed-blood' speakers are now in North Dakota, USA. The two languages involved in its formation were French and the Native American language Cree. Unlike Pitcairnese, Michif does not have very much simplification. We can guess that this is because of the greater involvement of young children in its formation than was the case for Pitcairnese. Children are, of course, much better language learners than post-adolescents and adults, and simplification mostly results from the imperfect learning of a source language by learners over the age of fourteen or so. Michif, in fact, is remarkable in that its noun phrases are French, complete with gender and adjectival agreement, while its verb phrases are Cree, including the complex verbal morphology of that language. For example:

la	fam	mičimine:w	li	pči
the (fem.) woman		she-is-holding-it	the (masc.) little-one	
French		Cree	French	

'The woman is holding the child.'

9. Language and Humanity

In previous chapters we have discussed a number of cases in which irrational attitudes and discriminatory decisions, often made by governments or other official bodies acting out of ignorance or prejudice, have led to language policies which have had detrimental effects on children's education and even on societies as a whole. We saw that the British government in the eighteenth century attempted to make the speaking of Gaelic illegal. We discussed the way in which nonstandard dialects of English, such as AAVE, have incorrectly been regarded as inferior or inadequate. We noticed the extent to which varieties of pidgin English were looked down on as 'broken English'. And we observed the political disadvantage at which speakers of minority languages can often find themselves.

Many other similar examples of prejudice and unreason could be given. In 1994, for example, a minister in the French government tried to outlaw the use of English words in French, on the totally erroneous grounds that the French language is under some kind of threat. Many languages are under threat, as we shall see below, but French is most certainly not one of them. There has also been a powerful political movement in the USA in recent years, known as the 'English only' movement, which has been attempting to exclude languages other than English from the educational, cultural and political life of many states. Some of the supporters of this movement argue that they are in favour of it because the position of English is being threatened. In actual fact, of course, of all the thousands of language varieties in the world, American English is the one which is most definitely the least under threat.

It is a sad but true sociolinguistic fact that language issues can bring out the worst as well as the best in human beings, and that some people who would otherwise pride themselves on being intelligent and rational can behave in the most illogical ways when it comes to language issues. One of the things that linguists in general and sociolinguists in particular have tried to do over the years is to encourage people to think in a more sensible way about language issues by providing them with more information about language. This is important for all sorts of reasons to do with fairness, equality and even the future of humanity. None of the irrational attitudes towards language we have just cited has any basis in fact, but they can have all sorts of unfortunate consequences.

One of the very distressing consequences that attitudes of this type can have is *language death*. One of the questions linguists are often asked is: how many languages are there in the world? This is a rather difficult question to answer, not least because of the dialect-versus-language issue we have discussed a number of times in this book. It is not too inaccurate to say, however, that there are about 5,000 languages in the world today. What is much more certain is that this number is smaller than it used to be and is getting smaller all the time. In the last years of the twentieth century, languages are dying out without being replaced at an increasingly catastrophic rate.

What happens is that communities go through a process of *language shift*. This means that a particular community gradually abandons its original native language and goes over to speaking another one instead. This has been a relatively common process in the sociolinguistic history of the world. Two hundred years ago, for example, most of the population of Ireland were native speakers of Irish Gaelic. Now the vast majority are native speakers of English.

Before the Roman conquest, the population of much of what is now France were speakers of the Celtic language Gaulish. Subsequently, however, they shifted to the language of their conquerors, Latin, which eventually became French. Later on, the northern part of France was conquered by the

Germanic-speaking Franks. These conquerors, however, eventually went through a process of language shift and ended up speaking French too. Similarly, the Norwegian-speaking Vikings who subsequently conquered and settled in the part of northern France we now call Normandy also shifted from their Scandinavian language to French. A few generations later, as a result of the Norman conquest of England in 1066, these former Scandinavians took the French language to England. Once in England, however, it took the descendants of the Norman conquerors only a few generations before they shifted once again, this time to English.

What is different about the modern situation, however, is the speed and the extent of the language shift which is taking place around the world. In most cases, moreover, language shift is leading to complete language death, the total disappearance of languages from the world. When the Normans stopped speaking Norwegian and shifted to French, Norwegian still survived in their Scandinavian homeland. But if Irish finally disappears from Ireland, which seems likely although not inevitable, then this will represent an instance of complete language death.

In Europe, a number of languages have died even in quite recent times. Cornish, for example, died out in Cornwall in the eighteenth century. And Manx, a close relative of Irish, lost its last native speaker on the Isle of Man in the 1950s. Many other European languages are currently under threat of dying out: Scottish Gaelic, Breton in Brittany, Frisian in the Netherlands and Germany, Sami in Scandinavia, Romansch in Switzerland.

In the rest of the world the problem is much more serious. In the Americas, for instance, at the time of first European contact in the fifteenth century, at least a thousand different languages were spoken. In the last 400 years, at least 300 of those languages have died out completely. Of the remaining 700, only 17 have more than 100,000 speakers, and only one of those, Navaho, is in North America. More than 50 languages have died in the USA alone since the arrival of Europeans.

In the Pacific Ocean area, the problem is probably even

more serious still. Perhaps as many as a quarter of all the world's languages are spoken in this area, and very many of them indeed are under threat. In Australia, for instance, there used to be about 200 aboriginal languages. Of these, 50 are already dead, and another 100 are very close to extinction. Perhaps as few as 30 will make it to the year 2000.

Linguists believe that this is a very serious problem, and that the preservation of linguistic diversity in the world should have a high priority in the same way that the preservation of biological diversity does. It is obvious, for example, that the connection between languages and cultures is an intimate one, and that the disappearance of languages from the world could greatly speed up the process of cultural homogenization. A monocultural world would not only be a very dull but probably also a very stagnant place. Languages as partial barriers to communication are probably also a good thing since they make it more difficult for the cultures of economically powerful and populous societies to penetrate and replace those of smaller communities.

Sociolinguists, most notably the American Joshua Fishman, have been active in trying to combat this process. *Reversing language shift* is an activity which requires considerable sociolinguistic expertise and knowledge as well as hard work and large sums of money. The aim is to help small culturally threatened communities to transmit their languages to the next generation. Money for nursery schooling using the mother-tongue can be vital. The provision of incentives and opportunities to use the language in everyday life is also important. And it is necessary for communities to understand that bilingualism is normal and beneficial and not some kind of aberration.

Perhaps even more important, however, are peoples' attitudes to languages. There are very many, often complex, reasons why language shift takes place. Frequently, though, people abandon the language which is the repository of their culture and history and which has been the language of their community for generations because they feel ashamed of it.

If rich and powerful people more technologically advanced than yourself tell you frequently enough that your language is inferior and backward, you may end up believing them and come to think that way yourself. If you also see that people who speak your language are treated unfavourably and discriminated against, then that too will obviously be a powerful disincentive against using it.

Such negative evaluations are of course not only made in the case of languages. They are also often made, as we have seen, in the case of dialects. Here, too, unfavourable and irrational attitudes towards nonstandard varieties are widespread. Although it makes no sense at all to claim that one variety of, say, English, is linguistically superior to any other, there are many people who believe that this is in fact the case and who act on that assumption. For example, in the English-speaking world, the variety of English used in schools is Standard English, while the language of most children, and working-class children to a greater extent than middle-class children, consists of various types of nonstandard English. Educational difficulties may obviously arise from this difference. One important factor causing such difficulties for working-class children, however, may be the unfavourable attitudes some of their teachers may have towards nonstandard dialects. Even if these attitudes are only subconscious, they can lead to unwitting discrimination in favour of children with middle-class accents and dialects. Evidence on this point comes from the work of social psychologists, who have revealed the extent to which people's speech can influence how they are perceived by the use of *matched guise* experiments. In these experiments, groups of subjects are played tape-recordings of, say, five different speakers, all reading the same passage of prose, and all with, for example, different accents of English. They are then asked to give their opinions on the five speakers, and it is explained that the investigators are interested in how skilled the subjects are at deducing things about the speakers' attributes and capabilities from their voices alone. Subjects may be asked, for instance, to locate speakers on scales ranging from 'very intelligent' to 'very unintelligent', 'very friendly' to 'very unfriendly', and so on. It is then often found that subjects show a high level of agreement in finding that, say, speaker 3 is more intelligent than speaker 2, who in turn is less friendly than speaker 4. The interesting point about these experiments is that two of the speakers are, unbeknown to the subjects, the same speaker – but the same speaker using two different accents. If, therefore, speaker 2 and speaker 5 are the same person, and yet speaker 2 is evaluated as being more intelligent than speaker 5, then this difference must be due to the different forms of language he or she was using. In fact, experiments in Britain have shown that speakers using an RP-speaking guise are generally regarded as more intelligent and more educated, but less friendly and less likeable, than the same speakers using a local-accent-speaking guise.

This illustrates the way in which we rely on stereotypes when we first meet and interact with people (as in a train, for example) and use the way they speak to build up a picture of what sort of person we think they are. RP-speakers may be perceived, as soon as they start speaking, as haughty and unfriendly by non-RP speakers unless and until they are able to demonstrate the contrary. They are, as it were, guilty until proved innocent. Similarly – and this is of course far more worrying – children with working-class accents and dialects may be evaluated by some teachers as having less educational potential than those with middle-class accents and dialects, unless they, too, are given an adequate chance to demonstrate the contrary.

Just as in the case of language death, so irrational, unfavourable attitudes towards vernacular, nonstandard varieties can lead to *dialect death*. This disturbing phenomenon is as much a part of the linguistic homogenization of the world – especially perhaps in Europe – as language death is. In many parts of the world, we are seeing less regional variation in language – less and less dialect variation.

There are specific reasons, particularly in the context of Europe, to feel anxious about the effects of dialect death. This is especially so since there are many people who care a lot about language death but who couldn't care less about dialect death: in certain countries, the intelligentsia seem to be actively in favour of dialect death.

It may not be immediately obvious that dialects are just as intimately linked to cultures as are languages. But just as there are national cultures, so there are local cultures, and dialects symbolize these local cultures and maintain and defend them. Indeed, in modern Europe it is possible to argue that, at least in some cases, local identities as symbolized by dialects are actually more desirable than national identities as symbolized by standard languages. In some situations, regional dialects, by reinforcing local cultures and local identities, may act as a counter to nationalism.

It is also necessary to point out to those who despise regional dialects that dialect death and standardization can actually cause rather than solve communication problems. This is particularly likely to be the case where there are geographical dialect continua. Take, for example, the border between The Netherlands and Germany. As we saw earlier (Chapter 1), this is a border without a dialect boundary. Speakers on either side of the border speak dialects which are the same or very similar. This has meant that for generations there has been ready and easy cross-border communication, as there continues to be today. Working-class Dutch people from Nijmegen, for example, travel across the border to the German town of Cleves to visit, to shop, and to work. Working-class Germans travel in the opposite direction. However, just as western European nations are breaking down barriers to cross-border travel and employment, middle-class Dutch and German people from Nijmegen and Cleves are no longer able to participate so readily in this cross-border traffic. This is because they can no longer speak the local dialect. If middle-class Dutch people who can only speak Standard Dutch want to travel to work in Germany, they have to study and learn Standard German because the people of Cleves cannot understand Standard Dutch. Many Dutch people have learnt Standard German, but many fewer Germans have learnt Standard Dutch. The dialect continuum which permitted easy communication has, at least for middle-class speakers, been cut and broken by standardization.

We have to acknowledge that much dialect loss in modern Europe is due to processes connected with geographical mobility and urbanization which are probably sociolinguistically inevitable. There is nothing we can or would wish to do about that. What we can work against is that kind of dialect loss which is the result of attitudinal factors. In most European countries, although the majority of the population do not speak the standard variety, they are discriminated against in various ways and made to feel that their native vernacular dialects are inferior, not only socially, which is unfortunately true, but also linguistically, which is most emphatically not true. It is hardly surprising, therefore, if many of them try to shift to the standard variety even if, at some level of consciousness, they do not really want to.

In this kind of atmosphere, traditional dialects or patois can disappear surprisingly quickly. Traditional dialects have more or less disappeared from most of England, for example – although not from Scotland – and in many parts of the French-speaking world the picture is the same. There is often, of course, a direct relationship between the degree of hostility to dialects and the rate at which they disappear. One way of combating this hostility is to point to those fortunate, more tolerant societies which do have greater respect for language varieties as good examples to be followed.

In many dialect-hostile parts of Europe, including England, there is a widespread view that dialects are out-of-date, old-fashioned, unsophisticated, divisive, economically disadvantageous. To combat this belief, we can point to the following fact. In 1990, according to many measurements of per capita income, the three richest countries in Europe were Luxemburg, Norway and Switzerland; all three countries are dialect-speaking.

As we saw in Chapter 5, the entire indigenous population of Luxemburg is dialect-speaking. They learn and use German and French, but their mother-tongue is Luxemburgish/Letzeburgish, which is widely regarded as a dialect of German.

Norway, too, is one of the most dialect-speaking countries in Europe. Some people do speak a form of Standard Norwegian, but the majority do not, whatever the social situation. People speak dialect on radio and TV, professors give lectures in dialect, and authors write poems and novels in dialect. The most important aspect of the Norwegian language situation, however, is, as we saw in Chapter 7, that there is an enormous societal tolerance for linguistic diversity and that, what is more, linguistic diversity in Norway is officially recognized and officially protected. This is most clearly illustrated by the fact that in Norway there is a law which states that teachers are not allowed to try to change the way children speak in the classroom. If children come into school speaking dialect, as most of them do, they must be allowed to continue to do so. (This provides an unfortunate contrast with Britain: in 1994, the British Minister of Education announced that all children should speak Standard English.)

Norway is also of considerable interest when it comes to attacking the denigration of vernacular varieties, in that lower-social-class dialect forms have quite deliberately been introduced into the Norwegian standard languages (see Chapter 7). Standard languages, that is, do not necessarily have to be élitist. Contrast this with what has happened in other countries. Just when, in the twentieth century, literacy in Europe was supposed to become universal, we have moved the goalposts by making literacy dependent on the acquisition of standard varieties based on upper-social-class dialects, and thus more difficult for most people to acquire. You may be able to write, but unless you can write the upper-class standard variety, it doesn't count.

Switzerland, too, is well known for its multilingualism and for its official and reasonably successful protection of four different language communities. However, the most interesting thing about Switzerland is that the majority of its inhabitants are dialect-speaking. In the so-called German-speaking area of the country, all the indigenous inhabitants are dialect speakers.

It would be too much to claim, of course, that Luxemburg,

Norway and Switzerland are rich because they are dialect-speaking. But we should not underestimate the degree of alienation that occurs in situations where people are denied the dignity of having respect accorded to their vernacular speech. Nor should we underestimate the advantages of having a population able to express itself fluently and clearly in its own vernacular, without having to monitor the extent to which they are speaking 'correctly' or not.

In contrast, in the English-speaking world there is a widespread but seriously mistaken assumption that dialects are made up of a series of 'errors' and that Standard English is somehow endowed with greater 'correctness' or 'clarity' or 'adequacy'. Dialects, it is believed, are 'inadequate' for certain tasks and cannot be used for educational or intellectual purposes. Similar views are held in many other places – France and Poland, for example. The Swiss German situation shows that nothing could be further from the truth. Of course, if you are to discuss a particular subject adequately, you need to be in command of its register – the vocabulary associated with that subject. But it is obvious that there is no necessary connection between dialect and register. This becomes clear if you hear two Swiss German professors discussing, say, the work of Heidegger using, of course, all the appropriate philosophical vocabulary, but employing also Swiss German dialect pronunciation and grammar. The same phenomenon occurs in Norway.

There are people in Britain who argue that all children should speak Standard English because those who are not able to speak it are at an economic and occupational disadvantage. This is sad but true. People who wish to become bidialectal (see below) must be given the opportunity to improve their chances in this way. However, this is not the same thing at all as arguing that everyone should at all times and in all places speak the same standard variety.

Besides, there is an obvious moral issue here concerning the human rights of dialect speakers. If individuals suffer discrimination as a result of racism, we do not suggest that they change their race, although of course in places such as the United States there is a long and sad history of black people doing their best to look as much like white people as possible. If individuals suffer discrimination as a result of sexism, we do not suggest that they change sex, although of course there are celebrated cases in history of women pretending to be men for various reasons. If individuals suffer discrimination because of the dialect they speak, then it is the discrimination that should be stamped out, not the dialect, although of course we cannot be surprised if, in the meantime, people try to protect themselves against discrimination by acquiring another dialect.

It is important to consider what we should do about dialect differences, and dialect prejudice, in schools. In Britain, probably as few as 12 per cent of children come into school being native speakers of Standard English. If we require or reward Standard English in the school system, the other 88 per cent are clearly going to be at some kind of disadvantage. What are we to do about the majority of children who are not native speakers of Standard English? So far it is possible to distinguish three different approaches that have been adopted to this problem. The first approach has been described as 'elimination of nonstandard speech'. In this approach, traditional in most parts of the English-speaking world and still quite widespread, every attempt is made in the schools to prevent children from speaking their native nonstandard varieties, and each nonstandard feature of which the teacher is aware is commented on and corrected. For example, the child will be told that it is 'wrong' (and perhaps even bad or a disgrace) to say *I done it, I ain't got it*, or *He a good guy*. Standard English, on the other hand, is presented as 'correct' and 'good' – the model to be aimed at. Pupils who attain proficiency in Standard English are often considered more favourably than those who do not.

Linguists, and many others, believe this approach to be wrong, for several reasons. First, it is wrong *psychologically*. Language, as we have seen, is not simply a means of communicating messages. It is also very important as a symbol of identity and group membership. To suggest to children that their language, and that of those with whom they identify, is inferior in some way is to imply that *they* are inferior. This, in turn, is likely to lead either to alienation from the school and school values, or to a rejection of the group to which they belong. It is also *socially* wrong in that it may appear to imply that particular social groups are less valuable than others. This is particularly undesirable when the language being stigmatized is that of lower-class black children and the one which is being extolled is that of white middle-class adult teachers. Finally, and perhaps most importantly, it is *practically* wrong: it is wrong because it does not and will not work. To learn a new language is a very difficult task, as many people know, and in many ways it is even more difficult to learn a different dialect of one's own language – because they are so similar, it is difficult to keep them apart. The fact must also be faced that, in very many cases, speakers will not *want* to change their language – even if it were possible. First, there are no communication advantages to be gained (as there would be in learning French, for example) since the child was already able to communicate with Standard-English speakers anyway. Second, the pressures of group identification and peer-group solidarity are very strong. Linguistic research has shown that the adolescent peer-group is in many cases the most important linguistic influence. Children do not grow up speaking like their parents, and they certainly do not grow up speaking like their teachers – their speech patterns are those of their friends. In other words, time spent in the classroom trying to eradicate nonstandard speech is wasted time. If children suffer because they speak nonstandard English, the solution is not to eliminate the nonstandard varieties.

The second approach has been called 'bidialectalism', and has received the overt support of many linguists. This approach teaches that the individual has a right to continue using a nonstandard dialect at home, with friends, and in certain circumstances at school. But it also advocates that children should be taught Standard English as a school language, and as the language of reading and writing. The two varieties, standard and nonstandard, are discussed and treated as distinct entities, and the differences between them are illustrated and pointed out as an interesting fact. The aims are to encourage the child's interest in language by study of his or her own dialect as a legitimate and interesting form of language, and to help the child to develop an ability in *code-switching* – switching from one language variety to another when the situation demands (something most nonstandard-English-speaking children are often quite good at anyway). This approach recognizes the appropriateness of nonstandard varieties for peer-group interaction and other functions, and respects childrens' feelings about their own language. For best results it requires that the teacher should have some knowledge of the linguistic correlates of social stratification, and of the child's dialect. It also concentrates solely on grammatical and vocabulary features. (Of course, it may be valuable to point out to children that some accents are more highly valued than others – but also that this is a social, not a linguistic fact.) It seems that this approach is likely to be successful, for the most part, only with writing, which is a more conscious and less automatic activity than speaking. In general, what the teacher does in the classroom with respect to spoken Standard English will probably be irrelevant – because of the social and psychological factors we have out-lined above. Children will learn to speak Standard English, which is a dialect associated with and symbolic of a particular social group in our society, only if they both want to become a member of that group *and* have a reasonable expectation that it will be possible, economically and socially, for them to do so.

The third approach has been called 'appreciation of dialect differences'. This view states that if children suffer because of their nonstandard language, this is due to the attitudes society as a whole, and perhaps teachers in particular, have to language of this type. If this is the case, then it is the attitudes that should be changed, and not the language. In other words, the problem is not really a linguistic one at all. We should, according to this approach, teach children to read Standard English, but, beyond that, we should simply attempt to educate our society to an understanding, appreciation and tolerance of nonstandard dialects as complex, valid and adequate linguistic systems. Critics of this approach have called it hopelessly utopian. Given time, however, it might prove to be simpler than the other two approaches, since it may be easier to change attitudes than to alter the native speech patterns of the majority of the population. Education towards tolerance could be carried out in schools – but only by teachers free from language prejudice (who may in the end find it more rewarding – and perhaps morally more defensible – than teaching Standard English). Supporters of this approach would hope, in the long run, for a situation where native speakers would no longer believe that they 'can't speak English'.

But what of the short run? As other critics have pointed out, in the short run we cannot afford to abandon the bidialectalism approach. Until the degree of tolerance at which the third approach aims has been achieved, children with no ability in Standard English will continue to be at a disadvantage. For this reason, to advocate the employment of the third approach alone may be to neglect the needs of these children. From the point of view of the linguist, therefore, the most satisfactory solution to the problem of nonstandard speakers in a Standard-English-dominated culture is the adoption in schools of a combination of the two approaches, bidialectalism and appreciation of dialect differences, bearing in mind that bidialectalism is likely to be only partially successful (and then probably only in the case of writing) and may be dangerous, particularly if insensitively handled, from the point of view of fostering linguistic insecurity.

If we are going to foster and preserve linguistic heterogeneity in the world – and it is of course precisely linguistic heterogeneity that is the subject matter of sociolinguistics – then we need all speakers of all languages and all dialects to be able to rest secure in the knowledge that their varieties of language are all amazingly structurally complex products of the human mind, of human societies, and of tens of thousands

of years of human history. And that all these varieties of
language are worthy of being passed on to the generations to
come.

Annotated Bibliography and Further Reading

Chapter 1

Useful introductory works to sociolinguistics include W. Downes, *Language and Society* (Fontana); J. Holmes, *An Introduction to Sociolinguistics* (Longman); R. Fasold, *The Sociolinguistics of Language* (Blackwell); R. Fasold, *The Sociolinguistics of Society* (Blackwell); R. Hudson, *Sociolinguistics* (Cambridge UP); J. Pride and J. Holmes (eds.), *Sociolinguistics* (Penguin); and P. Giglioli (ed.), *Language and Social Context* (Penguin). There is an emphasis on anthropological linguistics in D. Hymes (ed.), *Language in Culture and Society* (Harper & Row), which contains a paper by Haas on interlingual taboo from which I have taken some of the data used here, as well as in R. Burling, *Man's Many Voices* (Holt, Rinehart & Winston), where the full Njamal kinship data occurs. The writings of Sapir and Whorf in this area are to be found in D. Madelbaum (ed.), *Selected Writings of Edward Sapir in Language, Culture and Personality* (California UP), and B. Whorf, *Language, Thought and Reality* (MIT Press). Work on geolinguistics is discussed in J. Chambers and P. Trudgill, *Dialectology* (Cambridge UP), while secular linguistics is the topic of J. Chambers, *Sociolinguistic Theory* (Blackwell) and of W. Labov, *Sociolinguistic Patterns* (Pennsylvania UP). The influence of Labov's work can be noted in much of the present book, and his writings are both stimulating and important. Also recommended are his *The Social Stratification of English in New York City* (Center for Applied Linguistics = CAL) and *Principles of Linguistic Change* (Blackwell). Friedrich's study of Russian kinship terms is in S. Lieberson (ed.), *Explorations in Sociolinguistics* (Mouton).

Chapter 2

The results of the Detroit urban dialect survey led by Roger Shuy are not readily available in their entirety. Some of the results, however, including many of those I have used here, are set out in W. Wolfram, *A Sociolinguistic Description of Detroit Negro Speech* (CAL). The Norwich data can be found in P. Trudgill, *The Social Differentiation of English in Norwich* (Cambridge UP). Sociolinguistic methodology is discussed in L. Milroy, *Observing and Analysing Natural Language* (Blackwell).

Chapter 3

The topic of language and ethnicity is the subject of H. Giles (ed.), *Language, Ethnicity and Intergroup Relations* (Academic), and of J. Edwards, *Language, Society and Identity* (Blackwell). W. Whiteley (ed.), *Language Use and Social Change* (Oxford UP) contains a paper by Berry dealing with the Accra data, together with a number of other articles relevant to topics discussed in Chapters 5 and 6. Readers interested in Black English are referred to W. Labov, *Language in the Inner City* (Pennsylvania UP), W. Wolfram and N. Clarke (eds), *Black–White Speech Relationships* (CAL), and the more popular J. Dillard, *Black English* (Random House). American teachers and educationists are also referred to R. Burling's excellent *English in Black and White* (Holt, Rinehart & Winston), J. Baratz and R. Shuy (eds), *Teaching Black Children to Read* (CAL), and R. Fasold and R. Shuy (eds), *Teaching Standard English in the Inner City* (CAL). Books with a more British flavour are V. Edwards, *The West-Indian Language Issue in British Schools* (Routledge & Kegan Paul), and *Language in a Black Community* (Multilingual Matters), M. Sebba, *London Jamaican* (Longman), and D. Sutcliffe, *British Black English* (Blackwell).

Chapter 4

Jespersen's writings on this topic can be found in *Language: its Nature, Development and Origin* (Allen & Unwin), while the Koasati data is taken from a paper by Haas that appears in the Hymes reader (see Chapter 1 notes). Other useful references can be found in A. Capell, *Studies in Socio-Linguistics* (Mouton), and D. Crystal, 'Prosodic and Paralinguistic Correlates of Social Categories' in E. Ardener (ed.), *Social Anthropology and Language* (Tavistock). Good readers, with very useful and extensive bibliographies, are B. Thorne and N. Henley (eds), *Language and Sex: Difference and Dominance* (Newbury House), in which the Norwich study and references to the work of Lakoff can be found, and B. Thorne, C. Kramarae and N. Henley, *Language, Gender and Society* (Newbury House). Highly recommended is J. Coates, *Women, Men and Language* (Longman).

Chapter 5

Brown and Gilman's T- and V-pronoun article, 'The Pronouns of Power and Solidarity', and Ferguson's 'Diglossia' paper have both been reprinted a number of times. The former appears in J. Fishman (ed.), *Readings in the Sociology of Language* (Mouton), and the latter in the Hymes reader. Both also appear in the Giglioli volume. For those especially interested in style and stylistics, D. Crystal and D. Davy, *Investigating English Style* (Longman) is recommended, while a number of articles in J. Gumperz and D. Hymes (eds), *Directions in Sociolinguistics* (Blackwell) deal with aspects of the relationship between language and social context. Also relevant are J. Fishman, *Language in Sociocultural Change* (Stanford UP), S. Romaine, *Bilingualism* (Blackwell), and J. Gumperz, *Language in Social Groups* (Stanford UP).

Chapter 6

Aspects of the social psychology of language, including the study of the use of language in social interaction and the findings of matched guise experiments, can be found in H. Giles and R. St Clair (eds), *Language and Social Psychology* (Blackwell). The study of conversation is dealt with in M. Coulthard, *Introduction to Discourse Analysis* (Longman), and the more advanced M. Stubbs, *Discourse Analysis* (Blackwell), as well as in R. Wardhaugh, *How Conversation Works* (Blackwell), while readers interested in the ethnography of speaking can find a number of very readable studies in R. Bauman and J. Sherzer (eds), *Explorations in the Ethnography of Speaking* (Cambridge UP). A very useful general book is M. Saville-Troike, *The Ethnography of Communication* (Blackwell). The cross-cultural communication problem example is taken from R. Scollon and S. Scollon, *Linguistic Convergence* (Academic). The same authors have also produced *Intercultural Communication* (Blackwell). Some of Tannen's work can be found in D. Tannen, *You Just Don't Understand* (Morrow).

Chapter 7

The discussion of language planning in Malaysia is taken from R. Le Page, *The National Language Question* (Oxford UP). Many of the facts about the Norwegian situation can be found in a detailed treatment by E. Haugen, *Language Conflict and Language Planning: The Case of Modern Norwegian*. Good sources of information on problems of planning and standardization in different parts of the world include J. Fishman *et al.* (eds), *Language Problems of Developing Nations* (Wiley), R. Cooper, *Language Planning and Social Change* (Cambridge UP), and J. Rubin *et al.* (eds), *Language Planning Processes* (Mouton). For information on the linguistic situation in the English-speaking world, see C. Ferguson and S. B. Heath (eds), *Language in the USA* (Cambridge UP) and

P. Trudgill (ed.), *Language in the British Isles* (Cambridge UP).

Chapter 8

The English dialect data presented can be found in the publications of the Survey of English Dialects edited by H. Orton *et al.* and published by E. J. Arnold. The basic material is published in four volumes, each in three parts (i.e. twelve books in all): I. The Six Northern Counties; II. The West Midland Counties; III. The East Midland Counties and East Anglia; and IV. The Southern Counties. (These are best consulted in libraries.) More accessible information is available in M. Wakelin, *English Dialects* (Athlone), P. Trudgill, *Dialects* (Routledge), P. Trudgill, *The Dialects of England* (Blackwell), and K. M. Petyt, *The Study of Dialect* (Deutsch). The Tok Pisin data is taken from R. Hall, *Pidgin and Creole Languages* (Cornell UP). L. Todd, *Pidgins and Creoles* (Routledge & Kegan Paul) is an introductory text, as are L. Todd, *Modern Englishes* (Blackwell), and S. Romaine, *Pidgin and Creole Languages* (Blackwell). Bailey's data can be found in an article in D. Hymes (ed.), *Pidginization and Creolisation of Languages* (Cambridge UP). My 'Dutch–Swedish Pidgin English' example is based on a paper by Whinnom in the same volume. The subject of pidgins and creoles has become increasingly popular and well researched in recent years, and many valuable publications are now available. Among the most interesting is I. Hancock, *Readings in Creole Studies* (Story-Scientia). Bickerton's important book is *Roots of Language* (Karoma).

Chapter 9

Dialect in education is the subject of P. Trudgill, *Accent, Dialect and the School* (Edward Arnold), and W. Wolfram and D. Christian, *Dialects and Education* (Prentice Hall). J. Fishman, *Reversing Language Shift* (Multilingual Matters) is the seminal text in this field. Language death is the subject of

N. Dorian, *Investigating Obsolescence: Studies in Language Contraction and Death* (Cambridge UP).

Index

READ MORE IN PENGUIN

In every corner of the world, on every subject under the sun, Penguin represents quality and variety – the very best in publishing today.

For complete information about books available from Penguin – including Puffins, Penguin Classics and Arkana – and how to order them, write to us at the appropriate address below. Please note that for copyright reasons the selection of books varies from country to country.

In the United Kingdom: Please write to *Dept. EP, Penguin Books Ltd, Bath Road, Harmondsworth, West Drayton, Middlesex UB7 ODA*

In the United States: Please write to *Consumer Sales, Penguin USA, P.O. Box 999, Dept. 17109, Bergenfield, New Jersey 07621-0120*. VISA and MasterCard holders call 1-800-253-6476 to order Penguin titles

In Canada: Please write to *Penguin Books Canada Ltd, 10 Alcorn Avenue, Suite 300, Toronto, Ontario M4V 3B2*

In Australia: Please write to *Penguin Books Australia Ltd, P.O. Box 257, Ringwood, Victoria 3134*

In New Zealand: Please write to *Penguin Books (NZ) Ltd, Private Bag 102902, North Shore Mail Centre, Auckland 10*

In India: Please write to *Penguin Books India Pvt Ltd, 706 Eros Apartments, 56 Nehru Place, New Delhi 110 019*

In the Netherlands: Please write to *Penguin Books Netherlands bv, Postbus 3507, NL-1001 AH Amsterdam*

In Germany: Please write to *Penguin Books Deutschland GmbH, Metzlerstrasse 26, 60594 Frankfurt am Main*

In Spain: Please write to *Penguin Books S. A., Bravo Murillo 19, 1° B, 28015 Madrid*

In Italy: Please write to *Penguin Italia s.r.l., Via Felice Casati 20, I–20124 Milano*

In France: Please write to *Penguin France S. A., 17 rue Lejeune, F–31000 Toulouse*

In Japan: Please write to *Penguin Books Japan, Ishikiribashi Building, 2–5–4, Suido, Bunkyo-ku, Tokyo 112*

In South Africa: Please write to *Longman Penguin Southern Africa (Pty) Ltd, Private Bag X08, Bertsham 2013*

READ MORE IN PENGUIN

PSYCHOLOGY

Psychoanalysis and Feminism Juliet Mitchell

'Juliet Mitchell has risked accusations of apostasy from her fellow feminists. Her book not only challenges orthodox feminism, however; it defies the conventions of social thought in the English-speaking countries ... a brave and important book' – *New York Review of Books*

The Divided Self R. D. Laing

'A study that makes all other works I have read on schizophrenia seem fragmentary ... The author brings, through his vision and perception, that particular touch of genius which causes one to say, "Yes, I have always known that, why have I never thought of it before?"' – *Journal of Analytical Psychology*

Water Logic Edward de Bono

Edward de Bono has always sought to provide practical thinking tools that are simple to use but powerful in action. Here he turns his attention to simplifying the thought processes when dealing with practical problems.

Cultivating Intuition Peter Lomas

Psychoanalytic psychotherapy is a particular kind of conversation, a shared project and process in which both participants can express their individuality and negotiate their rights. Here Peter Lomas explores the aims and qualities of that conversation between therapist and patient.

The Care of the Self Michel Foucault
The History of Sexuality Volume 3

Foucault examines the transformation of sexual discourse from the Hellenistic to the Roman world in an inquiry which 'bristles with provocative insights into the tangled liaison of sex and self' – *The Times Higher Education Supplement*

Mothering Psychoanalysis Janet Sayers

'An important book ... records the immense contribution to psycho-analysis made by its founding mothers' – *Sunday Times*

READ MORE IN PENGUIN

PSYCHOLOGY

Introduction to Jung's Psychology   Frieda Fordham

'She has delivered a fair and simple account of the main aspects of my psychological work. I am indebted to her for this admirable piece of work' – C. G. Jung in the Foreword

Child Care and the Growth of Love   John Bowlby

His classic 'summary of evidence of the effects upon children of lack of personal attention ... presents to administrators, social workers, teachers and doctors a reminder of the significance of the family' – *The Times*

Recollections and Reflections   Bruno Bettelheim

'A powerful thread runs through Bettelheim's message: his profound belief in the dignity of man, and the importance of seeing and judging other people from their own point of view' – *Independent*. 'These memoirs of a wise old child, candid, evocative, heart-warming, suggest there is hope yet for humanity' – *Evening Standard*

Female Perversions   Louise J. Kaplan

'If you can't have love, what do you get? Perversion, be it mild or severe: shopping, seduction, anorexia or self-mutilation. Kaplan charts both Madame Bovary's "perverse performance" and the more general paths to female self-destruction with a grace, determination and intellectual firmness rare in the self-discovery trade. A most remarkable book' – Fay Weldon

The Psychology of Interpersonal Behaviour   Michael Argyle

Social behaviour and relationships with others are one of the main sources of happiness, but their failure may result in great distress and can be a root cause of mental illness. In the latest edition of this classic text, Michael Argyle has included the latest research on non-verbal communication, social skills and happiness, and has extensively revised and updated the text throughout.

READ MORE IN PENGUIN

LITERARY CRITICISM

The Penguin History of Literature

Published in ten volumes, *The Penguin History of Literature* is a superb critical survey of the English and American literature covering fourteen centuries, from the Anglo-Saxons to the present, and written by some of the most distinguished academics in their fields.

Sexual Personae   Camille Paglia

'A powerful book . . . interprets western culture as a sexual battleground pitting the Apollonian desire for order against the forces of Dionysian darkness' – *The Times*

The Anatomy of Criticism   Northrop Frye

'Here is a book fundamental enough to be entitled *Principia Critica*', wrote one critic. Northrop Frye's seminal masterpiece was the first work to argue for the status of literary criticism as a science: a true discipline whose techniques and approaches could systematically – and beneficially – be evaluated, quantified and categorized.

The Agony and the Ego   Edited by Clare Boylan

In this illuminating collection of essays, brought together to create a writer's workshop, authors as diverse as Patricia Highsmith, Fay Weldon, John Mortimer and Hilary Mantel discuss such aspects of fiction as inspiration, art and life, and the role of politics, plot and pleasure.

The Modern British Novel   Malcolm Bradbury

'Timely, acutely sensible and poignant . . . Bradbury delivers an overview of the evolution of the novel in Britain, turning over the tapestry of literary history and revealing the complex network of connections that lies underneath' – *Literary Review*

READ MORE IN PENGUIN

LITERARY CRITICISM

A Lover's Discourse   Roland Barthes

'*A Lover's Discourse* . . . may be the most detailed, painstaking anatomy of desire we are ever likely to see or need again . . . The book is an ecstatic celebration of love and language and . . . readers interested in either or both . . . will enjoy savouring its rich and dark delights' – *Washington Post Book World*

The New Pelican Guide to English Literature   Edited by Boris Ford

The indispensable critical guide to English and American literature in nine volumes, erudite yet accessible. From the ages of Chaucer and Shakespeare, via Georgian satirists and Victorian social critics, to the leading writers of the 1980s, all literary life is here.

The Theatre of the Absurd   Martin Esslin

This classic study of the dramatists of the Absurd examines the origins, nature and future of a movement whose significance has transcended the bounds of the stage and influenced the whole intellectual climate of our time.

The Art of Fiction   David Lodge

The articles with which David Lodge entertained and enlightened readers of the *Independent on Sunday* and the *Washington Post* are now revised, expanded and collected together in book form. 'Agreeable and highly instructive . . . a real treat' – *Sunday Telegraph*

Aspects of the Novel   E. M. Forster

'I say that I have never met this kind of perspicacity in literary criticism before. I could quote scores of examples of startling excellence' – Arnold Bennett. Originating in a course of lectures given at Cambridge, *Aspects of the Novel* is full of E. M. Forster's habitual wit, wisdom and freshness of approach.

READ MORE IN PENGUIN

POLITICS AND SOCIAL SCIENCES

National Identity   Anthony D. Smith

In this stimulating new book, Anthony D. Smith asks why the first modern nation states developed in the West. He considers how ethnic origins, religion, language and shared symbols can provide a sense of nation and illuminates his argument with a wealth of detailed examples.

The Feminine Mystique   Betty Friedan

'A brilliantly researched, passionately argued book – a time-bomb flung into the Mom-and-Apple-Pie image . . . Out of the debris of that shattered ideal, the Women's Liberation Movement was born' – Ann Leslie

Faith and Credit   Susan George and Fabrizio Sabelli

In its fifty years of existence, the World Bank has influenced more lives in the Third World than any other institution yet remains largely unknown, even enigmatic. This richly illuminating and lively overview examines the policies of the Bank, its internal culture and the interests it serves.

Political Ideas   Edited by David Thomson

From Machiavelli to Marx – a stimulating and informative introduction to the last 500 years of European political thinkers and political thought.

Structural Anthropology   Volumes 1–2   Claude Lévi-Strauss

'That the complex ensemble of Lévi-Strauss's achievement . . . is one of the most original and intellectually exciting of the present age seems undeniable. No one seriously interested in language or literature, in sociology or psychology, can afford to ignore it' – George Steiner

Invitation to Sociology   Peter L. Berger

Sociology is defined as 'the science of the development and nature and laws of human society'. But what is its purpose? Without belittling its scientific procedures Professor Berger stresses the humanistic affinity of sociology with history and philosophy. It is a discipline which encourages a fuller awareness of the human world . . . with the purpose of bettering it.

READ MORE IN PENGUIN

POLITICS AND SOCIAL SCIENCES

Conservatism   Ted Honderich

'It offers a powerful critique of the major beliefs of modern con-
servatism, and shows how much a rigorous philosopher can contribute to
understanding the fashionable but deeply ruinous absurdities of his times'
– *New Statesman & Society*

The Battle for Scotland   Andrew Marr

A nation without a parliament of its own, Scotland has been wrestling with
its identity and status for a century. In this excellent and up-to-date account
of the distinctive history of Scottish politics, Andrew Marr uses party and
individual records, pamphlets, learned works, interviews and literature to
tell a colourful and often surprising account.

Bricks of Shame: Britain's Prisons   Vivien Stern

'Her well-researched book presents a chillingly realistic picture of the
British sytstem and lucid argument for changes which could and should be
made before a degrading and explosive situation deteriorates still further'
– *Sunday Times*

Inside the Third World   Paul Harrison

This comprehensive book brings home a wealth of facts and analysis on
the often tragic realities of life for the poor people and communities of
Asia, Africa and Latin America.

'Just like a Girl'   Sue Sharpe
How Girls Learn to be Women

Sue Sharpe's unprecedented research and analysis of the attitudes and
hopes of teenage girls from four London schools has become a classic of
its kind. This new edition focuses on girls in the nineties – some of whom
could even be the daughters of the teenagers she interviewed in the
seventies – and represents their views and ideas on education, work,
marriage, gender roles, feminism and women's rights.

BY THE SAME AUTHOR

LANGUAGE/LINGUISTICS

Bad Language Lars-Gunner Andersson and Peter Trudgill

As this witty and incisive book makes clear, the prophets of gloom who claim that our language is getting worse are guided by emotion far more than by hard facts. The real truth, as Andersson and Trudgill illuminate in fascinating detail, is that change has always been inherent in language.

Our Language Simeon Potter

'The author is brilliantly successful in his effort to instruct by delighting . . . he contrives not only to give a history of English but also to talk at his ease on rhyming slang, names, spelling reform, American English and much else . . . fascinating' – *Higher Education Journal*

Grammar Frank Palmer

In modern linguistics grammar means far more than cases, tenses and declensions – it means precise and scientific description of the structure of language. This concise guide takes the reader simply and clearly through the concepts of traditional grammar, morphology, sentence structure and transformational-generative grammar.

The Language Instinct Steven Pinker

'A marvellously readable book . . . illuminates every facet of human language; its biological origin, its uniqueness to humanity, its acquisition by children, its grammatical structure, the production and perception of speech, the pathology of language disorders and the unstoppable evolution of languages and dialects' – *Nature*